The Golden Rules

Select Secrets for Winning at the Marketing Game

By **T.J. Rohleder**
"America's Blue Jeans Millionaire"

TABLE OF CONTENTS

INTRODUCTION

He Who Has the Gold...

We've all heard of the Golden Rule of social interaction. In theory, it goes like this: "Do unto others as you would have them do unto you." That's always a wise investment in the future... though cynics like to recast it as **"He who makes the Gold makes the Rules."**

Well, with this book, you've got an opportunity to learn the Rules that make the Gold—what I call the Golden Rules of Ruthless Marketing. So if your fondest dream is to make a fortune in the marketing field, then I hope you're not planning to put this book down and walk away anytime soon. Hidden inside it are time-tested, proven secrets you can use to make millions of dollars in the marketing field—as long as you're willing to study hard, learn the Rules by heart, and put them ruthlessly into play. **By "ruthlessly," I mean only in terms of how you treat your competitors; your customers and prospects are a precious resource that you should never mistreat or take for granted.**

If you've deliberately purchased this book or received it as a requested gift, then good for you! You've already got the right attitude, and that'll help you start rolling down the righteous path right away. If you're browsing through this book in a bookstore or library, then I urge you to buy a copy of your own as soon as possible. However you get your hands on a personal copy, once you've got it you can start highlighting, underlining, marking it up, attaching Post-It notes, dog-earing the corners, and otherwise making sure you can quickly **find and reread the Golden Rules that work best for you as you build your marketing empire.**

By now, you've probably wondering: Who is this guy, anyway? **T.J. Rohleder at your service. I'm President and co-founder of M.O.R.E., Inc., one of the nation's top direct response marketing companies,** which is located in the tiny town of Goessel, Kansas. **I know for an absolute fact that my Golden Rules work like a charm, because my wife Eileen and I used them to build our own fortune.** We started with $300 (that's three hundred bucks, not three thousand or three hundred thousand) and a dream, and in 20 years, we built that $300 into a company worth well over $100 million. **And the thing is, Eileen and I are just everyday, ordinary people.** The only thing that's ever distinguished us from the average Joe and Jane is that we decided a long time ago that we wanted to be rich, and then we just kept trying until we were.

We had our setbacks and difficulties along the way, sure enough. But we refused to give up. **I'm absolutely convinced that if we can do it, you can too, as long as you've got tenacity and that classic American can-do attitude.** I've formatted this book as an easy-to-follow guide filled with chapters of various lengths, mostly short, that you can pick and choose from as your business strategy requires—or as your heart desires.

Intrigued? Then turn to Chapter 1, and let's get started!

How to Make More Money by Doing Less Work

You might be shocked to learn that most entrepreneurs are losing huge sums of money, and even going broke, because of one simple error of judgment: they work far too hard. Oh, sure — to really, truly profit you *do* have to work hard. I told you as much in the Introduction. **But you have to work hard doing the right things, and in such a way that you also enjoy life...** because otherwise, what's the point? Just because you don't work 80-hour weeks to build your business doesn't mean you're lazy. It doesn't even mean you're going to fail. Hey, if you can make a fortune working 60, 50, even 40 hours a week (whatever the word "fortune" means to you), then you've found the golden secret to success, my friend.

But for those of us who haven't quite made it there yet, what's the starting point? How can you best cut your work hours back while still maximizing profit? **Easy: shift your focus to reselling to your best *existing* customers rather than forever scrambling to get *new* customers.** Many businesses ignore this strategy, which (to paraphrase Thomas Jefferson) I hold to be self-evident.

There are three, and only three, basic ways to build your business:

1. You can get more customers to seek you out and spend

money with you.

2. You can get customers to keep coming back to spend money with you.

3. You can get your customers to give you more money every time they buy.

That's it. It's nice to know that there are just three ways to build a business, since the process can be so frustrating and confusing. **Whenever you get too confused, always go back to the basics.** The place where most people go wrong is that they get stuck on the first method, constantly chasing after new customers.

But acquiring a new customer is like pedaling a bike up a steep hill on a hot day. It's tough, sweaty work, and you may have to get off the bicycle and walk it up the hill for a while. On the other hand, reselling is like coasting down the opposite slope of that hill. **Which would you rather do—pedal that bicycle up the hill, struggling the whole way, or coast right on down without moving a muscle, the wind ruffling your hair?**

Now, of course you'll have to conquer some hills before you can coast. So getting new customers is very important, but it's not everything. Never make that mistake of assuming otherwise. For some reason, far too many businesspeople fail to realize that all the profits are in the last two business-building methods I cited. **They're not building long-term relationships with customers, and they're certainly not making those people enough additional offers.** Because of all that, they're losing money that could be theirs.

New customer acquisition is a necessary evil for your business; otherwise, you can't utilize the other two methods.

But despite what some people seem to believe, as vital as it is, it's not the be-all and end-all of marketing. New customer acquisition should never demand a majority of your time, money, and focus. The best ratio is about 80/20—the old, familiar 80/20 rule. **Spend 80% of your time developing new products, services, and promotions designed to resell to existing customers for as long as possible, and spend 20% acquiring new customers.** If you shift up a little, say to 70/30, you'll leave your competition in the dust—but don't overdo it. Remember, the other two business building methods are where the real profits are.

You can see this easily in the restaurant business. Think of a successful restaurant in your community, one you've been going to for years. Chances are, the reason it's successful is because it has hundreds of repeat customers just like you. Personally, I have a couple of favorite Mexican restaurants I've been going to for over two decades now. **They appreciate the fact that I've been giving them money all that time. They treat me special,** doing everything possible to make me feel I'm wanted, appreciated, and valued. That's why I keep coming back, and why I tell all of my friends and family about those restaurants. I bring them with me, and then they bring *their* friends and family.

The same thing works for almost all businesses in every field. In a way, we're all in the restaurant business when we're in the business of reselling to existing customers. The world's most profitable businesses are set up to do that automatically on what's called a "til-forbid" basis—that is, **they're sold on monthly, bi-monthly, quarterly, or yearly contracts that automatically renew unless the customer cancels.** Those are the businesses with the highest resell value and the most profits.

If you're not in a business where you have a product or

service custom-tailored to be resold automatically, then you have to develop some. **You have to constantly keep your eye out for new and exciting things your customers will want.** You should always be thinking, "What's next?" **And in order to learn that, you have to build relationships with them and stay in touch.** I used to worry that I was trying to resell to my existing customers too often—that I might lose them because I was too aggressive with my marketing. I was like that throughout the first half of my business career... but that was *then*. Now I worry about the exact opposite—that I'm not trying to sell them *enough* new products or services. I realize now my that customers want to do more business with me, if only because we're all creatures of habit and want to do business with people we already like, trust, and have had positive experiences with.

That brings me to my next point, which is the fact that there is *so much* competition out there. Back when I used to worry about reselling to my customers too often, I didn't realize how oversaturated the marketplace was. The consumer of today has more choices than ever before. In my opinion, that's not a negative thing, and here's why: the more saturated the marketplace is, the more confused the average prospects will be. **Because of their confusion and the resulting frustration, they'll instinctively revert back to their habit of doing business with people they already know, like, and trust.** That's why you have to build relationships with existing customers, and do everything possible to bond them to you.

And here's another point to ponder: **your best customers are insatiable.** They want to buy more of the same kinds of products and services they've already bought from you, and there's a good chance they're already doing business with some of your competitors. So somebody is going to get their additional business. Why not you? It's your choice. **Oh, you don't have complete control over it, but you *do* have a lot of power in the relationship as long as you keep doing things to solidify that relationship.** If you do it well, they'll almost feel guilty if they do business with somebody else.

Your customer base is your meal ticket for life, as long as you handle them correctly. If you already don't have your customer list compiled on a computer spreadsheet so you can easily send out sales and promotional material to every last one of them, you have to do that right now. That has to be your first step toward building your fortune with marketing. Frankly, I'm shocked at the number of small business people who have no idea how many people are on their customer list—if they even have one. It's not possible for them to quickly mail out sales literature or a promotion announcement, and that's really sad.

Create a mailing list of all of your best customers, and segment it if you can. Spend some time thinking about this. Your best customers are the ones who've already bought the most from you—and generally, the people who've spent the most money with you in the past will spend the most money with you in the future. That may seem counterintuitive, but it's true. **When you segment your customer list, those people are the most important group. The next most important are the customers who've bought from you recently, because you know they have a serious interest in the products and services you sell. The third most important segment consists of people who bought from you a long time ago, but haven't made a purchase for a while.**

Focus on the first two groups, spending more of your time trying to get as many people as possible to keep coming back to you and spend as much of their disposable income on you as they can afford every time they buy from you.

You might say, "Well, where am I going to come up with all these great ideas for selling them additional products or services?" That's a great question; keep asking yourself that, and you'll come up with more and better answers. Personally, I get up at 5:00 every single morning and immediately focus on that question. I've been doing that for years. I think about my customers and about what they want the most. **I try to get inside their heads and hearts and really understand them in the most intimate way I can. I look at the products and services that have sold the best for us over the years, and I think about related items that I know they'd want to buy.** This is time spent working *on* my business, not *in* it. It's just me with a cup of coffee and quiet time in the morning, when there are no phones, faxes, or distractions. I'm able to focus on my business and my customers, and what I can promote to them next.

We strive to do 12-20 major promotions to our customer base every year. Depending on your business, that may seem like a lot to you or it may seem like a little; but in our case it involves a tremendous commitment of time, work, and effort. It's worth it, though, because that's where all the profits lie: in increasing the frequency that customers re-buy from you and then increasing the average profit margin per transaction.

If you focus on those two areas and maintain a new customer acquisition system that automatically brings in a steady flow of new customers, you're going to be light years ahead of your competition. You're going to make your competitors green with envy, too, because you'll be making huge profits by doing less work than they do. Reselling to people you already have a relationship with is like dealing with friends. In fact, we always personalize our letters that way, greeting them with, "Dear Friend." That's how we think about our customers. It's easy to do business with friends.

Here's another way to sell more products and services to your customers: hold special events for them. You can also invite new customers to these events. Now, this works better for some businesses than for others; but then, you can say that of any marketing example that I give you. I'm involved in a local pet boutique owned by my wife, Eileen. This is one of those upscale stores that sells premium food, treats, toys, and clothing for dogs; usually, they offer special grooming services and other services as well. Eileen holds an average of three special events a month to build relationships with her customers, and to encourage sales of higher ticket items. These events are usually small; sometimes as few as three or four people actually shall show up, and sometimes there may be as many as 12-20.

But she tries to make them fun, and most of her events are educational in nature. For example, she might bring in a veterinarian or dog groomer to give tips on how her customers can keep their dogs healthier or neater. A lot of her events are just crazy, informal things she ties into the seasons. You're limited only by your imagination here.

Eileen promotes her events through social media: she's on Facebook and Twitter, and has a website where she posts pictures of her customers and their dogs. **The events are excuses to re-invite people to come back into the store, and they give those people reasons to come back.** Even though only a small group might take advantage of a given event, each event is still important. Not only does it help her build customer relationships, it also sends a message to her entire customer base that says, "Here's a business that really wants to educate me on the ways I can improve the quality of my dog's life, and my life with my dog." **It's altruistic in nature, but at the same time, the more often Eileen can get people to come into the store, the more likely they'll purchase her dog grooming services and premium dog food—the two high-profit items she sells.**

And because Eileen always sends out a notice to the local media every time she schedules an event, **she gets a tremendous amount of free advertising.** Our newspaper and radio station love to announce her events, since they believe that keeping people aware of what's happening around town is a community service. So in addition to the regulars, new customers often show up too; and on top of that, word-of-mouth kicks in. Events like these are a great, dirt-cheap way of helping you stay close to your customers.

Never underestimate the power of altruism. Sometimes people will tune you out if it's obvious that you're staying in touch just to try to sell them something. But if you offer them a fun, non-sales event to take part in, they'll feel your business is different from all the others—that you care about more than just getting their money. And you should, even though your ultimate purpose is to make it easier for them to rebuy from you. **Solidifying your relationship with your customers is a crucial part of that process.**

So if you're worried about marketing too aggressively to your customers and chasing them away, as I used to be, hold more events like these. Find some excuse to invite them into your business to look at or learn something new, and make it fun for them. **Little promotional celebrations won't cost you money, they'll *make* you money.** Too many business people hesitate to hold such events because they're worried about the expense—but they're looking at things backwards. Done right, the benefits of small promo events far outweigh the costs, especially if you specifically invite only your best customers—that is, those who've spent the most money with you in the past. **These are the same people who are most likely to spend money with you in the future, particularly if you go to the effort to make them feel special.**

That's where all the profits are, and frankly, it's both fun and educational. **The more you try to build your relationships with your best customers, the more you'll enjoy them—and you'll also gain fantastic insight into the larger marketplace consisting of those who *could* end up becoming your best customers, if only you understood their wants, needs, and desires better.** That knowledge can be useful for future promotions.

Make an effort to spend more time with your customers, especially in non-selling situations where you can drop your guard somewhat, so they'll feel they're getting to know you better. **It's a simple strategy, effective because it combines salesmanship with the altruistic concept of serving the customer in the highest possible way.**

Write down those three main business-building methods and commit them to memory. Think about them daily. Anytime you're frustrated and confused about business, just return to the reality that there are only three ways you can build your business: by acquiring new customers, by getting existing customers to buy more, and by getting them to buy for a higher profit margin. That will help you understand what you have to do to make more money any time you feel you need to.

The more you realize that all your profits come from those two final business building methods, the more you'll your focus and energy into those methods. In the end, you'll work less, but make more money. And isn't that what it's all about?

Why You Must Be Lazy to Make Real Money

Believe it or not, you have to be kind of lazy to achieve major success. Don't believe me? **Look at it this way:**

Many small business owners try to do everything themselves, working themselves like dogs, and yet they never become financially independent. Often they go broke. One of the richest men that I've ever met once shared this pearl of wisdom with me: "The less I work, the more money I make." At first, I thought he meant that he was barely working at all, **but what he was really trying to tell me was that a small number of activities produce the most sales and profits. That's this secret in a nutshell.** If you'll strive to do the same, you can have an absolutely unfair, ruthless advantage over all your competition as you build your dream of financial independence.

First, you have to learn to focus. Second, you have to learn to delegate. Never do low-profit work that other people can do. Focus your energy on those few tasks that produce the most sales and profits. **In order to do that, you have to ask yourself: "What brings in the most money?"** Having determined that, you can then devote most of your time and energy to those few activities that produce the most profits. **Here are the four activities that bring in the largest amount of sales and profits in my business:**

NEW PRODUCT AND SERVICE DEVELOPMENT. I try to spend time every day working on new products or services. I'm always looking for ways to improve what we already offer, too. Every day I spend time on the phone with my Marketing Director, Chris Lakey, and/or my sales manager, Drew Hanson, or engaged in brainstorming sessions with key staff members doing exactly those things. We're constantly asking ourselves, "What's next? What can we do to top this? What can we do to make this better?"

CREATING NEW SALES MATERIAL. A significant portion of my day is spent rewriting old sales material to make it better, or to help sell new products and services in development. These sales materials are an integral part of our marketing system, which is our third big activity: **BUILDING THE MARKETING SYSTEMS. Marketing systems are complete processes dedicated to systematically attracting and retaining the largest number of the best buyers in our marketplace.** Marketing systems have many different components, each of which helps break down the sales resistance of our prospects, and helps educate prospects and customers as to why they should take action on our offers.

STRATEGIZING is our fourth crucial activity. I frequently brainstorm with myself and with staff members or joint venture business partners, constantly asking myself **"How can we do a better job?** How can we make our existing products and services even better, and develop future products and services that give the people in our market what they're searching for the most?" Some of this time is spent daydreaming and taking notes. Some I do while I'm watching TV at night. You can do the same.

By focusing on those four areas every day and letting

other people run the day-to-day part of my business, I'm doing less—but we're making more money, because those fewer things I'm doing are the things that make the biggest impact. Think about how you can devote more time to similar things.

Get good at delegating. Hire the very best people you can find: smart, bright individuals who fill the gaps in all the areas you're weak in. That's one sign of good leadership, and all modesty aside, I think I've matured into a good leader. I've surrounded myself with people who are bright and talented, very capable and competent, many of whom have been with me for a number of years now. They understand my business in an intimate sense; and in fact, each is very much a part of my business in his or her unique way. They work very hard at doing what they do, and I do everything I can to treat them with the respect they deserve.

This simple practice has been worth millions of dollars in sales and profits to my company. Now, I didn't always understand this; and there have been times when I've miscalculated my business strengths, and hurt the business as a result. My wife Eileen and I started our first mail-order business in 1988, and she ran the company until 2001. Eileen is the queen of common sense: she's very mature, very smart, and loved running the day-to-day side of the business—the part I hate the most. During those first 12 years or so, she let me focus my time and energy on learning the marketing side. I became a capable and confident marketer because she did such a phenomenal job of running the company. Then, in 2001, Eileen stepped down for health reasons.

That's when I stepped in as President and CEO of our company. Chris Lakey took my job as Marketing Director while I tried to fill Eileen's shoes. Well, I spent 2 1/2 years doing that—and in the process, **I learned that I'm the world's worst manager.** I have no business actually running a business; I just about drove the company into bankruptcy. When I realized that, I hired a business expert to come in and take over my company for 18 months. **He put a management team in place that remains with me to this day.**

That management team consists of *Chris Lakey* and my general manager, *Shelly Webster,* who's been with our company since 2000. Shelley has many of the same qualities that Eileen has. She's smart, detail-oriented, and very good at running the day-to-day part of our operation. *Randy Hamilton* stayed on as our bookkeeper/accountant, managing all the money. *Jeff McMannis* continued to run all our seminars and events. We hired *Drew Hansen* to build our sales department (which has transformed our business). *Felicia Crosby* runs our shipping, printing, and mailing house facility. Last but not least is my stepson, *Chris Bergquist,* who initially came aboard as our in-house graphic artist, and now is a valuable part of our management team.

Those highly talented people, as well as a select group of joint venture partners and loyal suppliers, have given me the freedom to focus all my time on those fewer activities that bring in the largest sales and profits. You must do that too. **The smartest thing you can do is work through other capable people.**

Either write that down, or print it and hang it up on your wall where you can see it every day.

GOLDEN RULE THREE:

How to Get More People to Give You More Money Right Away

The more you know about your customers, the more you can maximize your up-sells. In fact, **your ultimate goal should be to know your customers even better than they know themselves.**

You see, people often buy for unconscious reasons they themselves don't recognize. They aren't always aware of what they're *really* searching for in your marketplace, or what's driving them to buy a particular product or service. **It's an emotional thing, and most people are out of touch with their emotions.** So the more you think about your very best customers — who they are and the main benefits they're seeking — the more you'll understand them from that subconscious standpoint. **While it may be an unconscious process for them, it has to be a conscious one for you.**

Start by writing down a list of the things your best customers are looking for. As I've pointed out several times so far, they're the source of all your *real* profits. **Focus on who they are, and try to get to know them better.** One of the ways we've done that here at M.O.R.E., Inc. is by holding regular seminars and workshops for our customers. We've been doing this since September 22, 1990, two years after we started our business.

Now, let's be honest: the main reason we held that first seminar and the hundreds since was because we wanted to make more money. That was our #1 goal, and at first, we weren't thinking about anything else. **Our perspective has changed radically since then, because we've gained so much value just from the act of getting to know our customers better.** We spend a great deal of time every year face-to-face, belly-to-belly, eyeball-to-eyeball with them—and that's helped us more than we can measure.

Nowadays, we intimately know what our customers are looking for, what's most important to them, and what to say to them—and they don't realize it. When they come to our seminars, they don't see that our questions are designed so we can to get to know them even better, for our mutual benefit. We ask them what they're buying at the moment, and who they're buying from—all in an informal way, like we're just curious.

But we're taking mental notes that we later transfer to paper. **Our staff brainstorms constantly on the information our best customers have provided about the kinds of things they're buying the most from our competitors.** We're constantly asking ourselves, "What do they want that they're not getting?" We've learned that if you expect to get more people to give you more money right now, you have to intimately understand who your best customers are, and what they want the most.

So if you *really* want to maximize your profits, devote plenty of time to thinking this through. I suggest that you get up an hour earlier every day, like I do, and start trying to get inside the heads of your best customers. Forget all the rest. **A deep understanding of your best customers is where your true power lies as a marketer.** Ask yourself, "What's the #1 reason why my best customers are buying from me right now?" Then make a list of all the ideas that pop into your head. Write as fast as you can, and follow it up with other pertinent questions, like:

- What are they searching for the most?

- Why are they really buying what they're buying?

- What's the #1 one benefit they receive by giving me their money?

- What makes them excited about what they buy from my competitors?

The better you understand all that, the more power you'll have to attract other people just like them. Realize that your first answers to these questions won't always be the *right* answers, but they'll lead you to better answers. Sometimes it takes many months and years of thinking this through on a regular basis before you understand your customers better than they understand themselves.

Once you do start getting good answers to your questions, explore deeper. Another good question might be, "What are they not getting from me and my competitors?" **Here's the best question of this type I've ever heard; it's a fun question for brainstorming, and it goes like this. "In a perfect world, if I had god-like superpowers and I could give my customers anything that they wanted, what would it be?"**

Ask yourself that, then start writing down all kinds of goofy, crazy ideas. It's a wild and crazy question to start with, so the answers you come up with are going to be a wild and crazy, too. **Yet they'll help you think things through, so you can then find or develop products and services that come as close as possible to giving people the main benefits on your list.**

Make it fun. Keep thinking this through at a deep level. **This exercise serves you well, because the more you can do to understand your customers, the more power you'll have to get more people to give you more money.** Those people will include the best customers you have now, but you'll also end up attracting new customers similar to them—and your profits will increase dramatically.

The Cashflow Increaser, and How to Use It

Want to create a raging river of cash that keeps flowing and never stops? **The secret is to discipline yourself to keep plowing money back into the things that have already made you the most money.** Don't let the apparent simplicity of this statement fool you; this really can unleash an astonishing positive cashflow that gives you a major competitive advantage in your marketplace.

We've used this powerful secret to turn our business into a money machine. **Right from the beginning, we disciplined ourselves to put 30% of every dollar that we earned into new customer acquisition promotions, advertising, and similar marketing.** We actually kept two checkbooks, and made rigorous efforts to keep those accounts separate. Now, I had a good friend of mine who was inspired by our phenomenal success using the power of direct-response marketing; I told him a few of the main things to do, and he too had phenomenal success right out of the gate.

But he didn't hold back a marketing budget like he should have. Thousands of dollars came pouring in very fast—and what did he do? He leased an office building, bought new computer equipment, and spent it on infrastructure... and then he had no money left over for marketing. **He quickly lost his momentum and went out of business. Well, here we are still in business** two decades later, because we *didn't* make that mistake. We continued forcing ourselves to plow more money into the things that caused the money to flow to begin with.

Discipline is all about doing the things you *know* you should be doing. It's not easy, which is why there are so few people who practice it in all aspects of their life and business. But putting aside 30% of your income is an easy way to make sure you always have plenty of money to attract new customers and resell to your existing ones (which is all marketing really is.) **This simple secret has generated millions of dollars of sales and profits for us.**

We maintain a constant front-end marketing campaign that brings us a steady flow of new customers, and then we keep going back to our existing customers to do more business with them. That's all there is to it. Most small business people just don't understand that their best customers are insatiable. They'll continue to buy products and services as long as you continue to offer them, as long as those products or services are related to what they've bought from you the first time. But most small business people lose out on huge sums of money that could be theirs because they assume that their existing customers don't want to hear from them very often.

You can't make that mistake. **Your best customers *will* continue to buy more from you if you provide them the opportunity.** The reason they're more likely to buy from you (as opposed to your competitors) is because they already know you. They like you, they trust you, and they feel safer spending their money with you than with someone they don't have an existing relationship with.

So what are they insatiable for? Variations on a theme, really. **They're looking for the same things they bought from you the first time... only different.** Now, that statement is confusing to many people, but it's not as contradictory as it sounds. **You see, something about your new product or service has to be new, while underneath, it's very similar to what they bought from you before. In fact, it should include the same basic benefits.**

Test as many new ideas as you possibly can, in order to find what works the best. Then try to determine *why* that's working the best, all the while continuing to ask yourself, "How can I give my customers more of what they want the most?" I have a huge sign on the wall of the room where I do all of my creative work, and it simply says, **"Sell them more of what they want the most."** It sounds like comment sense, right? And yet as Mark Twain said, "Common sense ain't so common."

Remember: while people are always looking for something new, **if it's *too* new they won't be comfortable enough to spend money on it.** They're looking for things that have a veneer of newness, while offering the same general benefits they enjoyed before. Once you know what those benefits are (whether real or perceived) just keep finding or developing "new" items that offer the same benefits. **When you find something that really works and produces massive profits, try to incorporate it into as many of your future products and services as possible.**

This requires constant testing and tweaking as you search for what works the best. **It means keeping your finger on the pulse of your daily sales and profits, remaining extremely aware of where your biggest profits are coming from.** That's critical, so you can continue to give your customers more of what you know they want the most. **You know what that is not by what they're saying—they may not be able to articulate it themselves—but by where they're spending their money.**

Let your bestsellers guide you, and your business will evolve into a well-oiled money machine that cranks out a steady flow of dollars.

The Fastest, Easiest, and SAFEST Marketing System Ever

In this chapter, we'll take a look at the fastest, easiest, and above all *safest* marketing system I know of that still guarantees the most sales and profits possible. **This three-step marketing system is so easy a child can understand it... and yet none of your competitors seem to know about it. Here it is:**

1. Generate the highest quality leads possible.

2. Get those leads to request more information.

3. Follow up relentlessly with personalized sales material that pre-sells them.

Those are the only three steps. Now: read them again carefully. Do they seem simple? Indeed they are. But don't assume that they're *too* simple, because these three steps have generated a huge fortune for my own company, and for many others. **The good news is that they're safe. When you implement them correctly, they're very low-risk indeed. It's a proven moneymaking system.** Best of all, when you do this the right way, your competitors simply can't compete with you. Maybe that seems like a tall order for three simple steps—so let me show you just how simple it can be.

As I write this, we have two active front-end campaigns that utilize this three-step marketing system. **First,** we send a direct mail package to the best prospects in our market, offering them what we call a "free Discovery Package." In **Step #2,** a percentage of the people who get our direct mail package request our free Discovery Package, and we send it to them. In **Step #3,** we follow up with all kinds of additional sales material that encourages them to call our sales representatives to get all their questions answered.

When those people do call, they're already pre-sold and ready to buy—because the huge free Discovery Package we sent them does a phenomenal job of selling. Both our campaigns start with a small booklet (in one of the promotions the booklet is 24 pages long, and in the other it's 48 pages), along with an order form that lets them send for the Discovery Package. The Discovery Package itself includes a two-hour audio program, a 50-page portfolio (a sales letter in disguise), an eight-page question-and-answer summary (which answers all their biggest objections), and an application form (which is really an order form) for the initial service we're offering.

This simple three-step system is generating millions of dollars a year for us, so obviously it's not *too* simple. **The heart and soul of our free Discovery Package is that two-hour audio program,** where they can listen to us as we go over the 15 reasons why our service is exactly what they're looking for, and can therefore help them find everything they're searching for the most. Through that audio program and the associated written copy, we prove to them beyond any doubt that the service we're offering is worth far more in perceived value than the money we're asking them for. **Then they can call us and let our sales reps answer any other questions they have.** That's all there is to it.

That's how we ensure the best prospective buyers in the market come to us pre-sold. You have to create the same advantage for your own business, and you have to be willing to spend a little money in order to do that correctly. **The only thing that matters here is ROI—return on investment, which boils down to how much you spend vs. how much you make in the long run.** That's the *only* thing that's important.

As an example of how we use this three-step marketing system: 52 times a year we send out direct mail packages that contain the 24-page book in one campaign, and the 48-page book in the other. **Those books are just sales letters disguised as booklets... and we disguise them that way because while people love to buy, they hate to be sold.** What's the difference between buying and being sold? Simply this: the customer must feel that it's their choice to come to us.

In this context, a booklet looks friendlier.

The Awesome Power of Operation Money Suck

When used correctly, **this one Ruthless Marketing secret alone will double or quadruple your profits in no time flat**— and you can use it to make more money in less time than you ever thought possible.

Here's the secret of "Operation Money Suck": **you invest all your time, energy, and focus on every legal and ethical way you can conceive of that will allow you to extract the maximum amount of money possible from your marketplace.** Your goal is to be the dominant player in your market, to take the biggest slice of the pie for yourself.

You're surrounded by competitors who are aggressively going after the same people you're trying to sell to; if you don't get the prospect's disposable income, then your competitors will. **So you've got to get those people to come to *you* with their money, which means you have to be aggressive, ruthless.** Properly handled, your marketplace is your meal ticket for life. Therefore, from a metaphoric perspective only, **you have to view your competitors as the enemy.** Many of them can be your friends on your own time—but not when it comes to your overall marketing strategy and methods. That's one of the primary points underlying our entire Ruthless Marketing series.

As I outlined in the Introduction, **Ruthless Marketing has** *nothing* **to do with ripping people off.** Now, if you look at the dictionary definition of ruthless, you'll see that in some ways, it's a pretty evil word. But we don't mean it that way; **Ruthless Marketing simply involves being extremely aggressive in all of your marketing activities, so that you can maximize your market share.** You have to approach your marketing from the perspective that all that money could and *should* be yours. You have to realize at a gut level that your best customers really are insatiable, and that they'll continue to buy — if you give them the chance.

The harsh truth is that no matter how much they like and trust you, **if you're not trying to resell them on a regular basis, your customers will buy what they need from someone... so they might as well buy from you.** That has to be your mindset, your mantra. As a marketer, your job is to extract the most money you can from your marketplace. There's no reason to be ashamed of that; it just means you're doing your job well, that you're doing as much repeat business as possible while also doing everything you can to attract new customers.

Ironically, the best way to succeed as a Ruthless Marketer is to appear altruistic in the eyes of the marketplace. That's another of those apparent contradictions so common to Ruthless Marketing. It's not about ripping people off; **it's about helping them get more of what they want the most, and striving to give them what nobody else does.** There are *always* needs that are going unmet in your marketplace. It's up to you to figure out what they are. Your breakthrough ideas may not come to you for months or even years, but they'll *never* come to you unless you take the time to think deeply about this on a regular basis. **Your entire marketing strategy should be based on attracting more people like your best customers, and then doing as much**

repeat business as possible with them for the longest possible period of time.

Here's a quick story about how we once lost millions of dollars here at M.O.R.E., Inc. Everybody loves to hear our "rags to riches" story about how we turned $300 into over $10 million within our first five years, and how we went on to make over $100 million in our first 19 years...but they don't necessarily like to hear about how we've *lost* money. Yet I think such stories are important, because they illustrate how we made some serious mistakes in our early years. **In fact, during our first decade, we lost an untold amount of money that could have been ours if we'd just applied the basic principles of Operation Money Suck.**

Back then, we were still making the same huge mistake that so many other small business people make: our marketing emphasis was on acquiring new customers. We fully realized the importance of "replenishing the pond" by bringing in a constant flow of new customers... **but we didn't follow through very well.** Sure, we had follow-up products and services we tried to sell them, but we weren't aggressive enough in pushing those items—which cost us millions in earning potential. **We didn't realize then the majority of our profits had to come from repeat business.**

We've turned that around now. We now proceed on the belief that new customer acquisition is not the be-all and end-all of marketing, but rather a necessary evil, as I pointed out in an earlier chapter. **Yes, you need to generate a steady stream of new customers, but the process should be mostly automatic, so you can invest most of your time and energy on maximizing profits through Operation Money Suck.**

Let me reemphasize the fact that your existing customers are insatiable. They always have unmet needs, so you have to keep going back to the well.

I've mentioned that our new customer acquisition marketing system operates 52 weeks a year, systematically bringing in a steady flow of new customers. We also offer 12-20 major promotions annually to existing customers. Now, when you use direct response marketing methods, as we do, **all you need is a percentage of those customers to buy from you on a regular basis, and you can make big profits every single month, year after year.** Long-term ROI is all that really matters. All you have to do is make sure your overall customer base continues to grow, and you keep offering that growing customer base additional products and services related to the ones they've already purchased.

Here's the basic formula operating here, and I recommend that you think about it very carefully: **In order to make the largest amount of money possible, all you have to do is resell enough items, enough times, to enough people, for enough profit each time.** Commit that to memory. Write it on a 3 x 5 card you keep on you at all times. Hang it up on your wall. Think it through. Visualize it. Internalize it. Really understand what that formula is all about. It's as simple as it sounds.

Now, admittedly, within that simplistic formula there are many variables that make it exciting. Don't be overwhelmed by that. Whenever you get confused, just return to that formula, and you'll see how simple it is. **You must have an intimate knowledge of the real reasons why people buy the products and services you sell.** Here's an example. My primary business sells low-cost moneymaking business opportunities to people looking for ways to make extra money. There are millions of people in this market. If you ask, "What do these people want?" the superficial answers you'll get will be, "To supplement their incomes. To make more money by working fewer hours. To ensure a steady cashflow." **All that makes sense... but those answers are wrong.**

What the people in our market *really* want is a way to get rich quick. They want to be multi-millionaires. They're looking for an opportunity that will make them financially independent for life. They want to live in big houses, drive fancy cars, and take exotic vacations. They want to show off in front of their friends and neighbors. They want to be able to tell all the naysayers in their lives, "See? I told you so." They want to donate money to their favorite charities, churches, and communities, and they want to do all kinds of wonderful things for their families and loved ones.

We had to find that out the hard way.

I'll never forget our very first $5,000 seminar. We were nervous, because until then we'd stuck to low-cost seminars that sold for hundreds of dollars. Now we were going for the gold. The hotel ballroom was packed. It was a Friday night, and the seminar was set to continue until Sunday. We knew we had to kick it off successfully, so one of our speakers said, "Look: let's not tell them they can get rich overnight. Let's go down there and say, 'Just focus on making $50,000 your first year, and then try to double it your second year. Keep doubling every year, and eventually you'll make millions.'"

So that's what we did. I opened the seminar by saying, **"How many of you want to make $50,000 in your first year in**

business?" It got so quiet you could have heard a pin drop. The silence was extremely uncomfortable—and it looked like people were getting ready to bolt for the door. So, doing my best to think on my feet, I blurted, **"Now, how many people here want to make *millions* of dollars?"**

This time they all jumped up and started yelling and screaming, **and that's how we kicked off a wildly successful seminar.** They loved hearing that second question, because that was what they *really* wanted. Since our customers are clearly looking for the ability to get rich, we make sure that **every single moneymaking opportunity we promote to them has the potential to make them super-rich.** If it doesn't, then they just won't buy it—because that's the hidden benefit they're actually searching for.

Now, the truth is that many of them would be perfectly happy with an extra $2,000-$3,000 a month. Even so, that's not what their heart desires. **The hidden benefit is that they all want to get rich; they want their "caviar dreams" to be real.** That's what you have to sell as part of your Operation Money Suck. What do *your* customers secretly desire? What's the #1 benefit they're looking for? In a perfect world, if they could have anything they really wanted, what would it be?

You're never going to know the answer until you think deeply about what causes them to buy. Continue to ask yourself those questions. Look at your bestselling products and services. Befriend your customers. Pay attention to what they do. Get to know them. Question them. Find out what products and services your competitors are offering that they like the most, and then ask yourself, **"What is it about those things that makes their sales and profits shoot through the roof?"** Then try to incorporate as many of those elements into your own new products and services as you can.

That's Operation Money Suck in a nutshell—and **every day is Operation Money Suck Day.** See it as a game. Have fun with it. Play to win—and you can make more money in less time than you ever thought possible.

GOLDEN RULE SEVEN:

Turn Your Business Into a Money Machine

It will take some time and work to set this up in the beginning, but once you know the secret and put in the effort, you can just flick the switch of your brand new cash machine and watch the money come rolling in, almost effortlessly.

Here's the secret in a nutshell: you get rich using the power of leverage to create marketing systems that work for you automatically. Once you've invested the set-up time, work, and skill to develop them, they can stay in motion with very little effort on your part. **All you have to do to make you a ton of money with these systems is test carefully, let reliable people run them, and watch the numbers closely.** This really is the next best thing to having your own money machine that cranks out an endless flow of dollar bills, simply by attracting the largest possible number of the best-qualified prospects in your market, getting them to do business with you the first time, and then reselling to them again and again.

As you know, the definition of marketing is simple: it's all the things you do to attract and retain customers. You can set up systems to do all the attraction and retention for you. There are two basic types of marketing systems: front-end and back-end. The first attracts all the new customers you want. The second resells them automatically. **Once you build these systems, you can sit back and do little or nothing.**

These marketing systems can be very simple, or quite complex. Let me start by giving you an example of just how simple they can be.

I started my first business in December of 1985. It was a carpet cleaning business that consisted of me (a young man with only three months of experience in cleaning carpets), a beat up van (that I bought on credit for $1,000), and some old, broken-down carpet cleaning equipment (that I got on credit from a janitorial supply house). That was it. **I didn't have any money for traditional advertising,** like running ads in newspapers or on the radio or on TV, **so the only way I knew to get sales was to go knock on doors and offer to give people free bids for carpet and upholstery cleaning.**

So I went up and down Main Street in the small town of Newton, Kansas (population 19,000) and offered people bids. I knocked on thousands of doors. I printed up dirt-cheap flyers and put them on car windshields. Then, whenever I would do a carpet cleaning job, I would go around and talk to that person's neighbors on both sides of the street, to let them know I was cleaning their neighbor's carpet and to offer them a bid also. I made hundreds of follow-up phone calls. **I was willing to work within a 50-mile radius of Newton. That was my entire marketing plan.**

Prior to starting in the carpet cleaning business, I had been in sales for a couple of years, so I knew how to talk to people. **I booked an average of 15 jobs a week, which earned me a meager living.** But I was always looking for other ways to bring in business, especially because carpet cleaning is seasonal. In the wintertime, it was almost impossible to get people to let me clean their carpets; I had to knock on even more doors and talk to even more people to get less work.

I stumbled onto my first marketing system during my second year in business. It was so simple! It started when I went to a home show and paid a few hundred dollars for a booth. I put a little table up there, and my wife Eileen and I, along with my stepson Chris, gave everyone who walked by a flyer advertising our business. **Because we wanted to do a "show special," we also set up a shoebox with a slot cut in the top, along with a stack of forms people could fill out for a chance to win some free cleaning.** Whenever someone came by the booth, we simply said, "Please register to win three rooms of carpet cleaning or a chair absolutely free!" Little did we know that we had stumbled onto something big. Those who weren't interested just said "No" and walked on; only the truly serious, people who honestly needed some cleaning done, bothered to stop and fill out the form. **In other words, our prospects qualified themselves.**

Right after the show was over, we chose a winner — but we also had several dozen leads left over. So I called them back, reminded them that they had registered for our contest and that, while they hadn't won the grand prize, I could offer a consolation prize of a certain amount of cleaning for a reduced price. Well, people love to win; and we already knew they were serious about wanting their carpets or upholstery cleaned. When they found out they had won a "consolation prize," most were excited, and **I quickly converted one out of every three leads to an immediate sale.** A few said they weren't interested, and many of the rest said they weren't interested right now but told me to call them back later.

For almost three weeks after the show, I was booked solid. I had all the carpet and upholstery cleaning I could handle, and I was shocked at how easy it was to book all that work. **Those were the easiest sales I'd ever made in my entire life,** because prior to that, my closing ratio was about 1 out of 10 or 15. In other words, at best I got one out of every 10 carpet- and upholstery-cleaning jobs I tried for—and many of those weren't even immediate jobs. **Suddenly my conversion rate had jumped to one in three.** My first thought was, "Where are some other home shows I can set up in?" **But there were very few; so my next thought led me to my first real marketing system.**

I love Mexican food, and one of my favorite Mexican food restaurants was a little place in Newton called Lupe's. The way they served it was a little unusual: you had to stand in line at the counter waiting for your food, and when you got it, you could eat in or take it to go. Well, I ate lunch there 3-4 times a week; and one day I was standing in line thinking about how I could duplicate the phenomenal success I'd enjoyed at the home show. Suddenly, I had an inspiration: *I wonder if they'll let me put a contest box of some kind on their counter, because I'm a regular customer?* So I boldly asked them if I could do that, and they said, "No problem!" **They appreciated my repeat business, and were willing to do me a favor in return.**

It worked out well for me, because people who were bored with waiting in line would see my contest box, and if they were interested in carpet or upholstery cleaning, they would register. Every Friday afternoon I would pick up all the leads for that week, select a winner, and then I'd call up the remaining leads and offer them my consolation prize. The first few times I did it, I was as shocked and amazed as I had been right after the home show—**because again, my conversion rate was the same as before, about one in three, and most of those jobs were immediate.** The consolation prize was simple: if they purchased cleaning from me, I offered to add an additional room of carpet cleaning or free Scotchgarding, Scotchgard being protective coating for carpets or furniture. **Once I discovered this marketing system, my life was transformed.** Now the only doors I knocked on were those of my client's immediate neighbors, and the only phone calls I made were on Saturdays (except for customer service issues or word-of-mouth referrals). **I was working less and making more money!** Only later did I realize the dynamics that made this marketing system so profitable. It's simple, really: again, the only people who registered to win my contest were those who were ready and wanted to have their carpets and upholstery cleaned.

No longer was I marketing to everyone without any regard to their needs or self-qualifications. No longer did I close fewer than ten percent of my "leads." Now, I could spend a few hours every Saturday making a few dozen phone calls to the people who entered my contest, and I'd be booked up solid for the entire week. I never knew it could be that simple.

I didn't even call that a marketing system at the time, because frankly, back then I couldn't even define what marketing was. I just knew that I needed more new customers; and then once I got customers, all I had to do was call them back every few months to see if they needed additional work, or if they were still happy. That was *all* I knew. **After I invented my contest box system, I was still calling up my old customers on a regular basis, but now I had all the new customers I could handle.** This is an ideal example of a front-end marketing system, and after I realized how easy it could be to get new customers, **I vowed to never do without some sort of similar system again.**

You have to do something to get the highest possible

percentage of the best-qualified prospective buyers to take some form of action—to raise their hands and say, "Yes, I'm interested." In this case, the action I wanted them to take was to enter my contest. **Your new customer acquisition should be something specifically applicable to your kind of business.** Just make sure it's something valuable to the prospect. Your job as a marketer is to get qualified prospects to take one small step that leads to a bigger step, ultimately leading them to keep doing business with you for years.

Of course, my simple shoebox marketing system evolved significantly over the next 20 years. By the time I started dating Eileen in the late 1980s, I had become heavily involved in sending away for many different moneymaking plans and programs that were centered around direct response marketing (we called it mail order marketing back then). When Eileen saw all these programs I'd been sending off for, she asked me why I was so excited about mail-order marketing, and I told her it was a chance to make sales to people from coast-to-coast. **We could live right there in our little hometown of Newton, and do business with people all over the nation.**

Eileen fell in love with the idea of making money with mail order too, and we started working out a way to turn it into our primary business. **In September 1988, we started our first mail-order company with only $300.** We spent that $300 on a small ad in two national magazines I subscribed to. That ad told the readers about a special product we had invented, and then told them to call and listen to an amazing recorded message that would reveal the details. **The three-minute message was recorded on our answering machine, connected to the extra phone line at the farmhouse we were renting one mile outside of the little town of Goessel, Kansas.**

People who listened to the ad could request more information by leaving their name and address; then we shipped them the relevant information. That consisted of sales materials that sold them on our product. Once they purchased that initial product, we made them additional offers related to that first product. **Again, without realizing it, we had created a new, self-qualifying customer acquisition marketing system.**

That little marketing system ultimately brought in 160,000 new customers and generated a total revenue of over $10 million dollars in our first five years. We continued to learn everything we could about building marketing systems, and thanks to the help of Russ von Hoelscher, **we soon we began using direct mail. Once we did, our income just exploded!** Millions of dollars came pouring in during the late 1980s and early 1990s. Since then, we've spent two decades doing everything possible to master every aspect of building powerful marketing systems that attract and retain large numbers of the best customers in our market. We've tested thousands of different things over the years, and continue to look for ways to make our marketing systems even better.

All our marketing systems have this one thing in common: **Our front-end offers an initial information package for little or no money.** We do everything we can to make it as irresistible as we can. Once people send for that package, we put them through a series of follow-up mailings and let our sales reps go to work answering all their biggest questions, and otherwise doing everything possible to convince them that what we have for them is worth far more than the money we're asking in return. **When someone buys a product or service from us, they end up on our customer mailing list, and then we make them at least 12 new offers every year as part of our back-end.**

That's how simple it is—and it really does work like a money machine. The secret to making it work that way is to have a consistent promotion in the marketplace all year long generating new leads, which are then converted into sales; then we make additional sales with our back-end marketing systems.

These marketing systems are fun to build, and they can last for years—which is a good thing, because it often takes several months or even years to build all the steps of a particular system. **Once it's in place, it gives you a tremendous amount of power because you're making money automatically** (especially if you're letting someone else run it for you). You've made it easy for the very best buyers in your market to do business with you repeatedly. Even better, once you have a proven marketing system that automatically generates substantial sales, it's very easy to make minor adjustments to spin off new marketing systems that sell a wide variety of related products and services. **In other words, your ROI for that initial investment of time and effort is high, because you spend very little of both in adapting the system to the next product/service, and the next, and the next—just days instead of months.**

This really is the next best thing to turning your business into a money machine. It does take some time, effort, work, and energy in the very beginning in order to learn how to build a marketing system—but once you get that system in place, you can flip the switch and watch the money roll in almost effortlessly.

Seven Steps to Writing Killer Sales Letters

In this chapter, I'll provide seven secrets to writing sales letters that grab the prospect's attention, causing them to line up with money in hand, eager to trade it for what you have to offer. Does that idea appeal to you? I thought it might. This formula is simple, straightforward, and powerful. **Here's what you have to do:**

Step One: Start with the big promise.

Step Two: Paint the picture.

Step Three: Give them proof.

Step Four: Tell them why it's unique.

Step Five: Close your argument by telling them why they must act now.

Step Six: Make them a very special offer if they respond now.

Step Seven: End with a reminder of your promise and a strong call to action.

That's the basic blueprint of a great sales letter, from start to finish. Although there are other formulas, **this seven-step**

formula will empower you to write a letter that can potentially make you hundreds of thousands or even millions of dollars. No kidding: *one* sales letter can make you millions. I'm living proof. I've written and co-written a number of sales letters that have generated $1 million or more, and **if I can do it, then *you* can do it.**

Admittedly, formulas like this one are shortcuts... **but why *not* start with a shortcut to riches?** Sure, you can and probably eventually will spend years or decades mastering the art and science of direct response marketing; but that doesn't mean you can't earn while you learn. **By following these steps, and doing a few related things, you can make huge sums of money now.** I advise you to think deeply about each of these steps, both individually and collectively. So let's go over them in more detail.

STEP ONE: Start with a big promise. Brainstorm as many as you possibly can. When you finally can't come up with any more, **go back and review your list until you find the biggest and best promise.** That's the one to use.

STEP TWO: Paint the picture. Use vivid language to make it real in the minds of your prospects. **You have to get them to see what *you're* seeing.** Selling is always a transfer of emotion, so the more intensely you believe in something and the better you paint the picture of what you believe, the more real it becomes to your marketplace.

STEP THREE: Give them proof. You have to back up all your claims. Although selling is an emotional activity, **people need to justify their decision with solid facts.**

STEP FOUR: Tell them why it's unique. There must

always be something unique about you, your company, and your products or services; you have to differentiate or die. If you can't think of anything unique about your business or what you sell, then it's up to you to create that uniqueness. **So find or develop the points of differentiation important to your prospective buyers.** The more unique your product/service is in ways that are important to the marketplace, the more selling power you'll have—and the more people will be ready, willing, and able to give their money to you.

STEP FIVE: Close your argument by telling them why they must act now. People need good reasons not to postpone a decision to spend money. Remember, all your competitors (both indirect and direct) are trying hard to win the hearts, minds, and business of the same prospects you're after. You're just one of a crowd, which is why you must do everything possible to be heard above the crowd. **You have to create a sense of urgency, providing clear and compelling reasons why they *must* buy now.** If there *are* no such reasons, again, you have to create them—and make them sound credible. The more good reasons you give people to take action immediately, the more money you'll make.

STEP SIX: Make them a special offer if they respond now. This feeds into Step Five by becoming one of their biggest reasons for responding immediately. **Offer all kinds of free bonus gifts that are exciting and valuable to them, and emphasize that those things are *only* available for a limited time.** That will increase their sense of urgency.

STEP SEVEN: End with a reminder of your promises. Wrap it up with a complete summary of the offer, simplifying it as much as possible. **Make the strongest possible call to action,**

doing everything you can to persuade them to give you their money *now*.

It sounds like a lot of work, doesn't it? It can be; yet a good sales letter can make you tens of thousands, hundreds of thousands, or even millions of dollars. Doesn't that kind of ROI make it worth the investment? Isn't it worthwhile to spend a few weeks or months writing the most powerful and persuasive sales letter possible if you can make megabucks with it? Of course it is! **And don't assume that this methodology works only with direct mail, because this formula can also be used on a website, or in an audio or video presentation. Don't get hung up on the medium.**

Here's another tip. Part of the secret of creating a wildly profitable sales letter is to create long lists of as many different ideas as you can, think them all through, then write as much copy as you can before boiling it down to your best ideas. **Now, these best ideas will continue to evolve;** so while you're working on the first draft, don't worry about trying to format your sales letter. Write as much as you can as fast and furiously as you can. **Put your entire focus on communicating to the prospect why it's in their best interest to give you their money.** Boil it all down later, after you've got it all on paper.

This is the secret of the world's highest paid copywriters. Some direct response copywriters charge as much as $20,000-$30,000 to write one sales letter, and then they get as much as a 5% royalty on all the sales. Does that sound hard to believe? Maybe, but it's true. Smart marketers are more than happy to pay these copywriters enormous sums, because they know that a good sales letter can make them a fortune.

How do those copywriters do it? Just as I've already told you: **they write as much as they can and then boil it all down.** Some of my most effective sales letters started out as much as 100-200 pages long before being boiled down to as little as 12-24 pages. **Yes, I have written *hundreds* of pages of copy and then just taken little bits and pieces of the very best of the best and used them in my final sales letters.** Think about that. When you study powerful sales copy, please don't think that it *didn't* take a lot of time and work to achieve. It's our job to make it look easy!

The very first sales letter I ever wrote that made over $1 million took me over three months to write back in 1990. Some days I worked for 30 minutes; some days I worked for three hours, but I worked on it *every single day* of that three months. Then we mailed that sales letter to our customer base, and generated a fortune very quickly. Was it worth three months of my life? Absolutely! **Today I can do a sales letter like that one in three weeks, and is some cases as little as *one* week.** So even though it may take you a while to do your first few, you'll get better.

Like all marketing, writing top-notch copy that can make you rich is a skill you can learn. The formulas involved—like the seven-step formula I've just given you—are very important. Remember this: whatever produces millions of dollars for one person or company can make *you* a fortune, too. This formula has produced millions of dollars for us, which is how we know it can make millions of dollars for you.

Your goal, when you develop all of your sales materials, is to get people excited. Get their attention, and fan the fires of their desires. **Make them want what you have to offer, and prove to them that what you have can give them what they want the**

very most. I heartily encourage you to learn the skill of writing effective sales materials. It's fun, it's creative, it's challenging, and it's extremely rewarding. Oh, it can be frustrating at times; there's no question about that. It can take you years to learn how to do the most effective job—but don't let that stop you.

Here's how I learned this skill. I've mentioned that my wife and I started our first direct response marketing business back in September 1988, with two small space ads that cost us $300. It took me one whole weekend to write the tiny ad we ran in two national publications. I labored mightily over it. Why? Because it was the last $300 we had. I spent the whole weekend with an assortment of ads that I'd seen in the same publications we were planning to run ours in. I'd saved dozens of back issues of that magazine, so I cut out the ads I liked the most, spread them out in front of me, studied them thoroughly, and consulted them repeatedly as I wrote. I spent the whole weekend trying to incorporate the best themes and elements expressed in those ads into my own.

I can do that same ad in five minutes now. I'm not saying that to brag; it's just reality, because I've been doing this every day since 1988. But because we only had $300 to spend and needed to make a profit back then, and because I was new at the game, I took a whole weekend to write that ad—and **then I spent the next *eight weeks* writing the sales letter that went out to all the people who responded to that ad.** That's how long it took for those magazines to run our ad. I also spent that time working on an order form and developing the product itself, so I didn't work solely on the sales letter. **But I did work on it very, very carefully.** Again, I took all the sales letters I'd saved that persuaded me to buy similar products, and I incorporated he best ideas I saw into my sales letters.

That was my formula back then: I tried to model my copy on the best of the best of everything I saw other people doing. Thanks to the fact that I worked so hard on it, and to the fact that we had the right idea at the right time, **our $300 investment was soon bringing in an average of $16,000 a month. Then we met Russ Von Hoelscher—and within nine months, our total revenue shot from $16,000 a month to almost $100,000 a** *week.* That demonstrates the power of working with a marketing expert who knows what he's doing. Russ had over two decades of experience when he started working with us in the spring of 1989. He knew exactly what to do, and how to do it. The best of his knowledge and skills he transferred to us.

The one thing he did that made Eileen and me more money than anything else was that **he taught us how to write better ads and sales letters.**

Although I had written that tiny ad that got us started before we met Russ (along with the initial sales materials that sold our product)—**I desperately wanted to learn how to write truly effective sales copy.** So Eileen and I would pay Russ to come to our home occasionally and work with us for an entire weekend. He would fly in on a Friday night, and then spend the weekend helping us develop our products, services, and associated sales materials before flying back to California on Sunday. Russ wrote all his copy longhand. We always made sure that we had a big stack of legal pads and plenty of pens and Scotch tape on hand, because he would often cut out certain pages and tape them together. **When he left on Sunday, he'd leave behind a huge pile of legal pads that he had written sales copy on.**

During the course of that weekend, we'd sit around talking about all kinds of ideas for products and services that we could sell to our customers and prospects. At some point, Russ would get really excited and start writing as fast as he could; Eileen and I would sit there, shut up, and watch him create copy. When he stopped, we'd pour a fresh round of coffee, eat some donuts, and start talking about other ideas—and then Russ would do it again. He'd get all excited, he'd say, "Wait a minute!" and off he'd go. Sometimes he'd write for 10 minutes; sometimes he'd write for half an hour or even 45 minutes, occasionally asking us a question or two.

During those times, **I carefully watched how he transferred all his excitement and enthusiasm for the project to paper.** The following week, I'd take that huge stack of legal pads he left behind over to our typist, and she'd type them up. Then we'd do some minor editing to turn them into sales letters before sending those letters out to our customers, and then watch the money come in. It was the most amazing thing I'd ever done. **It changed my life forever.**

I desperately wanted to acquire those skills Russ had—the ability to get so excited about a product or service that I could write a sales letter that also got my prospects and current customers so excited they were eager to send me money. It was such a powerful, overwhelming experience to watch a true marketing master take the ideas that we came up with and transfer them onto legal pads, which were then transformed into checks and money orders via a little typing, some minor editing, and the U.S. Postal Service. **I wanted that power for myself, and was determined to get it!**

Thanks to the many conversations I had with Russ, I knew that this was a skill that could make us multimillionaires—if I could develop it on my own. So I worked at it every day for months. **Within a year of the first time Russ came to our home, I was able to create (with some help from Russ) our first sales letter that generated over $1 million.** I was hooked for life, and who wouldn't be? Think about how powerful it is to be able to take the ideas you come up with, and then use an advertising medium to literally turn them into money. Think how powerful it is to be able to so inspire people that they pull out their wallets, purses, and credit cards and give you their money in exchange for your words. It's the most powerful feeling in the world. It's addictive—and it's a skill that *you* can master.

I thank God that I had the opportunity to watch a master like Russ in action. So many people don't. He made it look easy to convert our brainstorms into persuasive sales letters—and in fact, it pretty much *was* easy for him. But remember: he had over 20 years of experience at the time. **Anyone who masters a skill can make it look easy; but in reality, it only becomes easy after you go through a very sharp, high learning curve.** Still, don't be afraid to go through that learning process, because learning how to write a good sales letter really can make you millions of dollars.

I'll admit that it can be very challenging and frustrating at times. Even though I've been doing this now for over 20 years, I still get frustrated. **I still run into challenges and roadblocks.** Anybody who tells you they don't is lying to you, no matter how experienced they are. Don't believe them for a minute. Sure, they'd love to convince you otherwise, because if you come to believe they have some special ability you don't have, they can convince you that it's best to give in and ask them to do the work for you. **The truth is that the skills they've learned to master have been acquired over a long period of time. You can develop the same skills.**

Remember that there are formulas to help you do so. **Start with the seven-step formula I've given you here.** This really is a powerful one. **Just dive in and get started, and proceed point by point.** Don't get hung up on trying to make your letter perfect from the word go; in fact, the best advice any marketer can give you is to write as much as you can as fast as you can during that first draft, not worrying about spelling, punctuation, or paragraph breaks during the initial creative process.

You have to keep the writing process completely separate from the editing and the rewriting process. During the writing process, your filters are wide open; anything is possible. You're totally focused on the prospective buyer or customer, trying to do everything possible to persuade them that what you have is worth much more than you're asking for in return. Your total focus is on them: on how you can provide the benefits they want most, and on how your product, service, opportunity, or self is completely different and so much better than any other available choice.

Lay out all the reasons why they must take action right now, and why it's in their best interest not to delay. **Do all you can to make them feel special and appreciated, as if your offer is unique to them and, at most, only a small group of others.** The more you can do this with your filters wide open, without thinking too critically and focusing on yourself and your needs, the better. How can you serve the customer in the highest possible way? How can you give them what you *know* they want the very most?

Later, after you've done everything possible to state your case in as many different ways as possible, stop and cool down. Come back with a relaxed mind, so you can carefully analyze everything you've written. **Try to determine which ideas are better than the others, and start boiling it all down.** I told you earlier that some of my best sales letters started out as hundreds of pages of copy; well, this was the exact formula I was using. I focused tightly on these seven steps. After I wrote those hundreds of pages, I reduced the copy to the best of the best. In some cases, I was able to hand off some of my copy to another experienced copywriter, who helped me with the final process.

While all this requires a lot of work, it can be a labor of love—something for you to get extremely excited about. **The first time you write sales copy that results in huge profits, you'll be hooked for life.** It's highly addictive because it's fun, exciting, creative, challenging, and rewarding. Just one sales letter can literally make you millions of dollars if the market is big enough, if the perceived benefits are big enough, and if you've done an effective job of convincing your prospects to buy. **Given the potential profits, mastering the skills of writing powerful letters, websites, ads, and other sales material is worth the all the time and effort you'll put into it.**

The world's most powerful people all share the common denominator of having the ability to influence large numbers of people. **That's the power that *you'll* have when you learn how to write truly effectively sales copy.**

The Awesome Power of Direct Response Marketing

One of the reasons why my wife Eileen and I made millions of dollars from the very beginning was because we studied every single aspect of direct response marketing we could find, and I learned how to write sales copy that went out into our marketplace and came back with cash and checks and money orders. **Back then, we didn't even accept credit card orders— and yet we *still* generated tens of millions of dollars in sales.**

In the previous chapter, I outlined my favorite formula for writing effective sales letters and related direct response marketing copy. In all, it took me eight long years before I started getting really good at it—and even so, we still managed to bring in millions of dollars with the copy I wrote. **At first, Russ von Hoelscher looked over all my sales letters and improved them; but I was determined to master this skill on my own.** I desperately wanted to learn how to write words that caused thousands of people to pull out their wallets and send their money to us. So I wrote all the initial ads that we used to launch our direct response marketing business.

When it came time to develop our own full-page ad, I worked for weeks on the copy before I gave it to Russ to review. He rewrote parts of it and created a brilliant headline, which was probably what made the ad so successful. **That one ad alone went on to generate hundreds of thousands of dollars in pure profits for us.**

I'll never forget what Russ asked me: "Why didn't you just let me write that ad for you?" **I answered him, "Because I wanted to learn how to do it myself." I knew from the beginning that that was the secret to making millions of dollars—and it can work for you as well as it worked for me.** In the last chapter, I also told you about the privilege and the pleasure I enjoyed of watching Russ write some of our sales copy—and how that sold me on the concept like nothing else could. Those simple, busy weekends were worth far more to us than the $2,500 each we originally paid Russ, and I believe that Russ too has since earned far more than that from our weekends spent together back in the tail end of the 1980s. Watching the copywriting process firsthand inspired me; and **once I wrote my first million-dollar letter, I was hooked for life.**

I want to re-emphasize that my skills didn't emerge full-blown. It took me years of hard work and constant practice before I felt I was good enough to write all the sales letters for our new customer acquisition programs, because **new customers are so much more difficult to sell to than existing ones.** I started writing copy on a daily basis back in the late 1980s, and here I am well over two decades later, and I *still* write copy every day. This has made us millionaires—and it has the power to do the same for you.

The best part is that you can earn while you learn. Frankly, you don't have to be a brilliant writer to create effective direct response sales copy for your best customers. **They already like you, trust you, and want to do more business with you. So just write to them; that's the best way to learn.**

Put your heart into learning this special type of alchemy, because that's precisely what it is. **It allows you to transform ordinary paper and ink into gold, leaving you financially set for life.**

The Self-Qualifying Widget

Every great marketing system must include some kind of "widget," as I like to think of it, that your prospects can send for on the front end. **This is crucial because it gets them to raise their hands and qualify themselves; and in so doing, it breaks the ice and warms them up for the sale.** As any salesman can tell you, cold calling sucks. So right from the beginning, you must do something to take away the prospect's fear, to loosen them up and get them ready to buy. This is your widget's job.

Here's a powerful example of how one company uses this concept. A chain of 23 furniture stores on the East Coast gets prospects to send for and answer a 20-question questionnaire they call their *Decorating Personality Profile*. In response, the company sends them a little personality profile based on their answers. This Profile breaks the ice with the prospects and prepares them for the next step. It makes the process fun for them, giving them a reason to take action and qualify themselves as interested parties (because those who aren't interested won't fill out the survey). This begins the relationship-building process that leads to the initial sale. The company then stays in touch with those people and does everything possible to get them to take the next step.

As you can see, your widget doesn't have to be complicated. Here at M.O.R.E., Inc. we offer all kinds of low- and no-cost widgets that make it easy for our best prospects to take that initial step. For instance, with our current front-end promotion, the prospects are asked to send for a free Discovery Package that includes a detailed 50-page portfolio, eight-page Q&A summary, and a two-hour audio program describing the special products and services we have to offer. **On top of all that, they get a free gift. Our Discovery Package is our widget.** Thousands of people request it every month, and in the end we generate millions of dollars in sales from those people.

The widget must be altruistic in nature, although admittedly it's intended to attract people to spend money with you. But there's no obligation. **It has to be cheap or free, something your best prospects will find appealing and valuable.** The whole point is to make it painless for folks to send for your initial package, so you can build your mailing list and start developing what, ideally, will turn into a long-term, mutually beneficial relationship. Remember how simple that furniture chain's *Decorating Personality Profile* is — and that's earning the, a cool two million in profits every year.

Once you've distributed your widget and your prospects have responded positively, all you have to do is aggressively follow up with them. **Do everything possible to get them to take the next step. Now, remember: that step is almost always the hardest,** so don't make the mistake that so many other small businesses make, and try to get them to take too big a step. Small steps offer less risk. Using a little widget to get people on your list is the best kind of small step, because where's the risk?

At most, they may lose a few bucks if they're unhappy; and even then, **you can make it up to them by implementing a simple, no-questions-asked guarantee.** If they're happy, great! They've qualified themselves by inviting you in. **You can then stay in close touch with them, making all kinds of additional** offers in an attempt to get them to take that all-important big step.

This could lead to millions in sales and profits, immediately separating you from your competitors who are *not* using this powerful technique.

Why You Absolutely, Positively Do NOT Want Happy Customers

As you can tell from title, **this Golden Rule goes directly against the grain of almost everything you've ever been taught about marketing—and yet it will be worth a fortune to you once you know it well and can deploy it successfully.** You have to understand a couple of universal facts about humans in order to understand how and why this works, namely: **1) People buy in a vacuum; and 2) Happy people don't pay the rent.** Every psychologist knows the latter, and builds his or her practice on it.

Many of our clients ask us, "What's the fastest, simplest, and easiest way to make millions of dollars?" Or, "What products and services can I sell to make me millions?" We always tell them, **"Don't focus on the products and services. Focus on the markets."** In a nutshell, a market represents any group of people with something in common that causes them to buy certain types of products and services.

So if you want to make millions, look for huge markets full of people with enormous problems. Then learn as much as you can about those problems, and find or develop products or services that solve them. **To put it bluntly, you're looking for a very unhappy group of people who are in physical or emotional pain, so you can alleviate their pain in return for their money.** You can see how this secret gives you the potential to make a mint.

You also want customers who are insatiable—people who will repeatedly buy from you for years. The last thing you want are customers who are fully satiated, because then there's no need for them to come back and do more business with you. Again, some markets are better than others—but still, you'd be surprised at the huge numbers of insatiable customers in many markets. The marketplace I've spent over two decades serving is just such a marketplace. **The business opportunity market is made up of millions of people who are unhappy and just can't sate their desires.**

These folks continually seek new ways to make money—and many become addicted to the process. Because there are millions of people in this market, our company has worked very hard for over two decades to understand these people in the most intimate possible way. As a result, we've been able to generate tens of millions of dollars in direct response marketing sales.

There are plenty of other markets filled with insatiable people who continually purchase and repurchase products and services that they hope will fulfill their desires. Think about where you can find such a market. **Where do huge numbers of people have major problems that are causing them some form of physical or emotional pain, pain that they're actively trying to alleviate?** Then focus on finding and developing products and services that can help them.

This one simple idea can literally be worth millions of dollars to you.

Ten Easy Things You Can Do Right Now to Quadruple Your Profits

Sometimes it takes very little to produce a surge of profits, and in this chapter, I'll discuss ten easy ways to do so. Don't let the ease or simplicity of these strategies fool you. **Together, all ten can easily *quadruple* your profits, and smart marketing covers them all.**

1. Give people what they want the most.

2. Develop products and services that appeal to a specific market.

3. Make sure those items have the largest profit margin possible.

4. Develop marketing systems that identify the right prospects and communicate the right message to them.

5. Reach and sell to those people as fast as possible for the largest profit.

6. Profitably resell to them as often as possible.

7. Create sales messages that build strong bonds with your customers.

8. Position yourself so you seem unique.

9. Create marketing strategies that allow you to control the selling process.

10. Make specific offers to your customers on an on-going basis, compelling them to come to you instead of waiting for them to come on their own.

All marketing should cover these key areas. Let's go over them in more detail.

Step 1: Give People What They Want

People buy what they want, not necessarily what they need. If folks only bought what they needed, then we'd all be living in mobile homes and driving beat-up used cars. Obviously, that's not the case. **Your job is to give people what they want**—and you have to think about that constantly. Keep asking yourself that, keep trying to answer, and your answers will improve with time.

Write down the answers you come up with and think them through. **Study your biggest and most successful competitors to determine what sells best for them, and ask yourself why.** What are they doing to give the people in your market what they want? How can you do a better job?

It can take a while to really understand what people truly want. The reason is simple enough: as I told you in the last chapter, **most people buy in an emotional vacuum, which means they can't always tell you what drives them. Therefore, you have to learn to read between the lines, which requires you to become very familiar with your customers and prospects.** Spend time with them, analyze the bestsellers in the marketplace, and continue to ask yourself over and over, "What is the attractor factor behind those products and services that causes the sales to spike? What are the people in my market really searching for when they purchase them? What are they looking for that they're not getting? Where are the gaps?" Keep digging deeper.

Remember, your job is to give people what they want the most but aren't getting anywhere else. The more time you spend thinking all this through, the better your answers will be—and then you'll be able to find and develop the products and services that put you well ahead of your competitors.

Many of your competitors are committing what I call marketing incest, merely following the follower—a case of the blind leading the blind. They're all performing the same marketing activities and copying each other point by point. There's nothing innovative, bold, or revolutionary in their product lines or sales copy, because they refuse to ask themselves the difficult questions I've outlined above. **So when you *do* ask and answer those difficult questions, and do so long enough, your answers will lead you to the development of cutting-edge products and services that the market will go crazy over**—the subject of our next step.

Step 2: Develop Appealing Products and Services

The key to this step is the word "develop." It means that you must constantly be at work. Success requires a consistent evolutionary process of trying to improve your offerings to make them better and more attractive to the specific market you serve. **You should work on product development every day, even if only for a few minutes here and there.** Keep a legal pad or notebook with you, or maintain a computer file that you regularly update. Document new ideas as they occur, and keep asking yourself the kind of high-quality questions that lead to high-quality answers.

Step 3: Maximize Your Profit Margins

Often you can add valuable services to the products you sell, and those services can be where all the real profits lie— because they give you a competitive edge. Another very powerful idea that you can use to increase your profit margins is to develop a variety of informational products and services as part of your overall mix. **Information is extremely valuable—and yet the profit margins are phenomenal.** Because of that, you can charge super-high prices that your best prospects and customers are more than happy to pay, thereby generating the largest profits possible.

Step 4: Get the Right Messages to the Right People

No matter how hard you market, you won't make a dime if you don't create marketing systems that efficiently and automatically communicate the right messages to the right people. A good marketing system simplifies this process, so the very best prospects will take some initial, self-identifying action that allows you to focus your efforts on them. **It then takes additional steps to get them to re-buy from you for years— and in some cases, decades.** When you systematize your marketing this way and keep tweaking it toward perfection, it can work like a well-oiled machine 24/7/365. You'll never have to pay it overtime, either, and it works on holidays and weekends.

Step 5: Reach and Sell to Your Prospects as Fast as Possible

Speed is essential, because good direct response marketing can be very expensive. This huge expense isn't a problem if you're applying Step 5 effectively. **It's very important that you reach and sell to the very best buyers in your market as fast as you can to achieve the largest possible profit right away.** This creates the positive cash flow you need to build your business.

Step 6: Resell to Your Customers As Often As Possible

Remember, the key to making millions of dollars is getting a large group of people to re-buy enough of your most profitable products/services enough times. It's as simple as that. **You must develop a plan for reselling to them as often as possible, offering as many additional related products and services as you possibly can.** To do that, you've got to really focus on Step #7.

Step 7: Build Strong Bonds with Your Customers

Your ultimate goal must be to develop long-term relationships with your customers that make it easy for them to choose you and your offers above every other choice they have. This requires a lot of thinking on your part, especially about how to position yourself and your company, and what you sell that separates you from all the competitors who are *also* doing everything they can to attract the people you're after. To accomplish this, you have to focus on the next step.

Step 8: Position Yourself So That You Seem Unique

If you asked 100 marketing experts to define what marketing is, you'd get 100 different answers. And yet all those experts would agree that good marketing is all about differentiation. **You** have to separate yourself from every other choice your prospects have; and to do that, you must seem unique. Notice the word "seem" here. Many people get nervous when they hear about this principle, and the first thing they say is, "But there's *nothing* unique about me or my products or my company." That may very well be true, in which case it's up to you to create that uniqueness. **Again, in order to do that, you have to know what's most important to your prospects. Then you can develop offers and marketing messages they find attractive.** That becomes your point of differentiation that leads the very best prospects to you and keeps them coming back.

Step 9: Create Offensive Marketing Strategies

You want to control the selling process as much as you can, especially on the front end, so start thinking offensively (in the sporting sense). Follow up with back-end systems designed to persuade your very best customers to come back and do more business with you. **Don't just wait for them to come and find you, or for them to come back once they do. Go out and get them!** How do you accomplish that? You use the final step on our list.

Step 10. Make Specific Offers to Your Customers on an On-Going Basis

This final step takes your prospects and customers by the hand and (gently) compels them to come to you. In direct response marketing, we don't really sell products and services; **we sell offers.** And what is an offer? Obviously, the core is the product or service you're selling, **but it also consists of special prices, bonuses, guarantees, other services they can purchase**

for a special price, special sales, and anything else you can use to induce them to take action and buy from you now instead of later.

You have to understand that all of your prospects and customers will do everything they can to put off making a buying decision for as long as possible. They know the value of their money, so they're trying to hold onto it as long as they can. **To get them to spend their money with you, you have to make them very attractive offers. So start piling it on.** Do everything possible to build a tremendous amount of value, until the money you're asking them to give you in exchange seems small by comparison.

To see a good offer in action, watch infomercials: those 30-minute TV shows that sell a variety of products and services. They do the best jobs of making powerful offers; they just keep stacking it up, don't they? "You'll get this and this and this, plus if you take action today you'll get this and this and this, too. But wait, there's more! The next 100 callers get free shipping, and we'll super-size your order! And all for $19.99!"

◆◆◆◆◆

Good offers can be structured in many different ways, but they all have one thing in common: **they do everything possible to persuade prospects and customers to take action right away, not later.** So think deeply about all ten of these individual steps and how you can implement them in your marketing plan, because they're all very important parts of the process. Now, don't be overwhelmed by this; it can take a lot of time and work to develop it all. **Start by getting on the other side of the cash register, examining the situation from the perspective of the**

marketer you are, not just as a consumer.

As you become a more serious student of marketing, you'll see common denominators used over and over by a wide variety of companies, which will help you identify the "secrets" behind their success. **The good news is that you have a lot of sharp marketers to study and learn from; even better, the strategies and methods they're using are very transferable.** In other words, you can use those same means to achieve your own profitable ends.

So put your thinking cap on, **think all this through—and you can quickly quadruple your profits, and then go on to generate more money than you ever dreamed possible.**

GOLDEN RULE THIRTEEN:

The Golden Key

There's one "golden key" solution to nearly every business problem you'll ever face—and yet most of your competitors seem totally blind to it. The secret's not a secret at all, or at least you'd think not. **It's simply this: More sales will solve almost any business problem.**

Obvious, isn't it? Just make more sales, and more profits will follow. **So why do so many businesses lose sight of this one basic reality?** Maybe they're just so busy expecting everything to be difficult and complex that they've somehow forgotten Business 101. Don't ever let that happen to you.

Here's a key idea for you to focus on and commit to memory: *Nobody ever went out of business because their sales and profits were too high.* There might have been a few extreme exceptions, but they're very much the exceptions. Usually, the opposite occurs. **The number one reason why small businesses fail is because they don't bring in enough sales to cover their overhead expenses and pay their owners a substantial income.** The owners end up working too many hours for too little pay; that wears them down, eventually they can't take it anymore, and ultimately they go out of business.

A positive cash flow, on the other hand, makes up for a multitude of sins. That's why it's the golden key to growing your business and paying you what you're worth. **So how do you accomplish it? Simply through better marketing.** The late, great business guru Peter Drucker once said, **"Everything in your business is an expense except for two things: innovation and marketing."** Innovation and marketing go hand-in-hand. Marketing, of course, is all the things you do to attract and retain the largest possible group of the best possible customers within your marketplace, and then get them to spend as much money as possible.

So how do you do that? Simple. **You devote your life to studying everything you can about all aspects of marketing.** It sounds like an extraordinary amount of work, and indeed it is. And yet it can also be a labor of love, and I mean that most sincerely. **I know from personal experience that you can derive a tremendous amount of satisfaction from this learning process.** It can be just as fun to implement what you've learned and see the proceeds roll in. Whoever said "money can't buy happiness" was right in some ways, but the pursuit of money *can* buy happiness. **Marketing is all about the pursuit of money.**

Part of that pursuit involves honing your understanding of marketplace psychology. Learn everything you can about what makes your customers and prospects tick. What's most important to them? What are they searching for the most that causes them to do business with companies like yours? What are they finding the least? Where are the marketplace gaps that need to be filled, and how can you create irresistible offers that make it virtually impossible for them to not give you their money?

That's one of the greatest questions that drives *me* on a daily basis: **how can I create the most irresistible offers possible, ones that my best prospects and customers simply cannot refuse?** This question keeps me up at night. Am I crazy? No! I'm passionately in love with marketing. It's the ultimate challenge.

The best marketers I know are like mad scientists, totally obsessed with finding new means of attracting and retaining the very best repeat buyers in their market. **They see it as a magnificent game in which you keep score with money, not work in the way that most people think of work.** It's challenging, yes, but it's also creative, rewarding, stimulating, exciting, and purposeful. It enriches their lives—and the lives of their employees, suppliers, joint venture partners and, last but not least, their loved ones.

Don't let the old "love of money is the root of all evil" attitude stop you. I agree with that, but it's not what I'm saying here. **I'm telling you to fall in love with the game of marketing, not the money itself. The money will follow if you can effectively maintain and increase your sales.** Just strive to be the very best in your marketplace. How can you rise above your competitors? How can you make them green with envy? What can you do to be #1 one in your market? What can you do to steal the best customers away from your competitors? How can you build such strong bonds of trust with your customers that they'd feel guilty if they took their business elsewhere?

The process of inventing answers to these questions represents a good part of what makes this golden key attitude so challenging and stimulating. So when I say that the secret to bringing in massive sales and profits is to devote your life to mastering marketing, I'm not talking about a ton of backbreaking, mind-numbing work. **I'm talking about something that gives you energy instead of taking it away. Ultimately, it's very rewarding in ways beyond the financial.**

Just remember: in a normal free-market economy, nobody goes out of business because their sales and profits are too high.

In fact, those are the companies that become the marketplace leaders everybody else tries to emulate. **Your job is to become such a leader, to strive to be the very best, to attract and retain superior customers and keep doing the most business possible with them for the longest period of time.** If you make that your number one priority, you'll gain a huge amount of market power *and* personal satisfaction— and you'll solve almost every business problem you're faced with.

Touch Their Hearts *Before* You Grab for Their Wallets

Every politician understands and uses this secret, and you can begin cashing in with it immediately. You have to realize and remind yourself that **you can't move people into action before you first move them with emotion; the heart comes before the head, so that's where you'll need to direct your primary selling message.** It's just another means of aggressively going after the money in your market in the most effective way possible.

Yes, this is a Ruthless Marketing principle; but again, Ruthless Marketing isn't about ripping people off or cheating them in any way. **You have to honestly offer them good value for their dollar. But to get them to buy, you have to penetrate the shell of cynicism they've erected to protect themselves and their money.** They've been preyed upon too often to immediately believe what you tell them. So take that into account, and accept the fact that all selling is emotional, not mental. People buy for emotional reasons first, and then back those reasons with logic.

When you take those two factors as your basic premise, it's easy to see why it's so important to win their hearts before you can win their wallets. But for some reason, **most small business people just don't realize how skeptical, cynical, and apathetic even the best prospects are.** The market is over-crowded and over-hyped, folks. There are too many competitors trying to get their money, and there's not enough to go around. So marketers start hyping it up with bigger and bolder promises... and prospects start to tune out all advertising messages. Suddenly, it takes much more effort to win someone's business. **Once you realize that emotion is the easiest way to reach them, you can begin to build your case as to why they should give you their money on a regular basis.**

Assume that all prospects expect your sales materials and salespeople to hype up your products and services, and that they believe very little (if anything) of what you're saying. Even if they do believe you at some level or in some details, you still have to begin from the standpoint that they don't.

I call this principle "starting with a negative premise to gain a positive result." You just presume your market's best prospects and customers don't trust you one bit—that they think you're lying, and that even *you* don't believe your own promises. **This is a real dilemma for marketers, because big, bold promises are the heart and soul of almost every advertisement.** Your entire marketing message *has* to be that way, so that what you're promoting is perceived as new and exciting. A strong element of hype is unavoidable if you're to pierce through the thick walls of sales resistance—that combination of cynicism, doubt, and apathy designed to keep you out.

On one hand, bold hype is what it takes to get people's attention. On the other hand, as soon as people feel you're misleading them or over-hyping your promises, their doubts and fears will take over—and doubtful people don't buy. **So how do you gain their trust while simultaneously hyping your products and services enough to get their attention? It's a delicate balancing act, and you can't achieve it by aiming at their wallets first.** This is probably the biggest challenge that most marketers face on a daily basis.

Here at M.O.R.E., Inc., our primary business is selling business opportunities—and we've been doing pretty well at it for over 20 years now. There are literally *millions* of people in the United States alone who are searching for powerful ways to make as much money as they can while spending as little time on the endeavor as possible. **They've got full lives to lead as it is; so those things that work best for them are proven opportunities that let them work less and earn more.** What they're really after is the one opportunity that's going to set them up financially for life, just like one roll of the dice might pay off big in Las Vegas or Atlantic City.

The problem is, the opportunity market is over-saturated, with thousands of competitors offering a wide variety of low-cost solutions. So all our competitors are hyping it up more and more to get the attention of this huge market. **That's our response, too—because we realize that while our prospects are always looking for something revolutionary and cutting-edge, we've still got to penetrate their shell of advertising indifference and somehow be heard above all the other shouts.**

Our very best prospects are on all the mailing lists, so they're always finding letters, postcards and flyers from individuals and companies selling low-cost business and moneymaking opportunities in their mailboxes, real and virtual. **Every competitor is hyping it up more than the next, because they know prospects are more likely to respond to things that sound exciting and different.** And yet, those same people are also extremely cynical, having built up a tremendous amount of sales resistance that causes them to mistrust people who actively seek their business.

That why we've developed this particular principle. We try to touch their hearts before we grab their wallets. **We try to move them with emotional messages that convince them that what we have for them truly *does* live up to its claims.** We show them they can trust us; that we're different from and better than all those competitors they've had poor experiences with in the past, the people who stimulated their sales resistance in the first place. We've succeeded in making tens of millions of dollars in our attempts to do so.

Our marketing does two things: 1) We look for the biggest and boldest promises and claims we can legally and ethically make—things that pierce through that initial sales resistance and separate us from all our competitors. **2)** We go to work like a team of highly paid defense attorneys busily proving that their client is not guilty of the crimes for which they've been charged. **We strive to create a preponderance of evidence that prove the business opportunities we offer are even better than we claim they are.** We do everything we can think of to take away the doubts and fears our average prospect has.

To do this, we create offers with built-in risk reversal that stacks the benefits in their favor, not ours. And we simply assume they don't believe a damned thing we say. That's our foundational premise. We assume they've been lied to, cheated, ripped off, and abused by other promoters, because that's all too common. It makes our job harder, and we have to be constantly above reproach. **That's why we create the most iron-clad guarantees we can: to eliminate every bit of risk, thereby winning their trust as we *prove* to them, rather than just *say,* that we're everything we claim we are—and more.**

Are we 100% effective at this? Hardly. We still lose more

sales than we gain, and yet that's perfectly fine because all we care about is our ROI—how much money we're making overall vs. how much money we're spending on our marketing. **With that in mind, we're willing to spend a lot of money on the follow-up marketing necessary to win the hearts and minds of the people we're trying to sell to.** We do that to provide them with a wide range of truthful, rock-solid reasons why our business opportunity is the one they've been searching for all their lives, and therefore the only logical choice they can make.

We strive to do everything possible to let them know we're the real McCoy; that they can trust us and that we'll be there for them every step of the way; so that when they do decide to get started with one of our business opportunities, they have zero risk. **If for any reason, or even no reason, they're not 100% satisfied with every aspect of our business opportunity, they can ask for and quickly receive their money back in full.**

This isn't just a Ruthless Marketing principle. As I mentioned earlier, every good politician knows you have to win the hearts of your constituents before you win their votes. So a good politician makes a huge number of promises that people want to hear, adjusting those promises based on the group he's in front of at any given time. **They know it's an emotional game— and they know they have to back up their promises with the most logical plan of attack possible** (because, of course, most people don't trust politicians any more than they trust salespeople or marketers).

Again, to do your job of winning the hearts and minds of the most people in your marketplace, **you have to start with the premise that those people are extremely apathetic and skeptical.** They have an incredible amount of built-in sales resistance that causes them to distrust everything you say. **When you start with that premise, you can immediately apply strategies designed help to break down those walls of skepticism.** Over time, you can thereby build a large customer base of people who will keep doing business with you for years— even decades.

GOLDEN RULE FIFTEEN:

Make Your Customers Chase YOU!

How would you like for people to happily, even gratefully, stand in line to give you most of their disposable income? That might seem like an impossible dream, but you can arrange it. All you have to do is get your prospects to chase you, rather than vice versa. **In the marketing field, whoever's being chased has all the power in the relationship.** The chasers have an air of desperation about them; we've all seen it. Well, desperation is a position of weakness, *never* an attractor factor.

In order to get people to chase you, you have to make yourself chaseable. That is, you have to arrange some combination of factors that they find very attractive about you, your company, and your products or services. There are plenty of things you can do to accomplish that, and in this chapter, **I'm going to give you three overall strategies to work with.** As you'll see, all three tie together quite neatly.

The first strategy is Two-Step Marketing, where your goal is to separate out the people who best fit your offer. Step #1 is to send out a marketing message; it can be through direct mail, the Internet, TV, radio, whatever. The medium isn't as important as the strategy itself. You just start with a low-cost or no-cost offer to the marketplace you serve, one that your best prospects will find attractive. This causes them to raise their hands, self-qualifying themselves by saying, "I'd like to learn more." **In Step #2, you follow up with that smaller group of prospects who have identified themselves.**

With this approach, you're essentially asking people to take some type of action to prove to you that they seriously want the benefits provided by your product, service, or company. This approach works like magic, because it lets you focus your advertising budget on your follow-up marketing activities within that smaller group of better prospects. **It also makes those people feel as if they sought you out, even though you made the initial offer.** Selling is an emotional game, and in their excitement, the best prospects will forget that you attracted them with your sales copy in the first place.

Therefore, they perceive that they're choosing *you* rather than you choosing *them*. **That's essential to the selling process, because once they start chasing you, you have a real advantage over them.** Think about all the times when you've been high-pressured by some salesperson. It made you want to run away, didn't it? Well, forcing someone to run away from you is hardly advantageous to the marketer. It smacks of desperation. **Remember: people love to buy things, but they *hate* to be sold.** What's the difference? Very simple. **When someone buys something from you, the perception in their mind is that they've chosen you, rather than you pressuring them.** This makes all the difference in the world, allowing them to exercise the power of choice. They want to buy things they choose rather than having someone chase after them, begging them to buy.

The more you understand the dynamics of Two-Step Marketing, the more you'll see that it's a superior strategy. **It lets you build a mailing list of the finest, best-qualified prospects, people who are most likely to end up becoming your very best**

customers and clients. It lets you do a more effective job of building relationships with that self-qualified minority, because it lets you spend more money on each person — which makes it easier to convince them that your product is worth far more than the asking price.

The second strategy is to become an expert in your market. Authority is one of the six basic factors of influencing people. Most of us are raised to respect authority. We listen to what the authorities say; their opinions matter more to us than anyone else's. **So *you* have to become an authority, and expert, in order to take advantage of that tendency.** This is a great way to separate yourself from your competitors, since it helps you convince your prospects that you can give them what they want the most. **The good news is, it's easy to become an expert.** The hard part is convincing yourself that you *have* to. Once you get past that, the process can be fun, fulfilling — and extremely profitable.

When your prospects perceive you as an authority, they'll not only gravitate toward you, they'll spend more money with you more quickly, and will continue to do so. Your prospects are more confused and frustrated than ever, given the overcrowded, over-hyped world we live in. For them, the good news is that they have more choices than ever before; the bad news is that all of those choices have left them feeling overwhelmed.

What do people do when they feel all this pressure? **They look for the fastest, easiest way to relieve their emotional pain. One of those ways is to find an expert.** They place great value on the opinions of anyone they perceive as a true authority — which is why they're willing to give their money to those who rise above the crowd and take bold actions proving their expertise. Experts in every field have loyal fans who chase after them every day. Some even have to hire people to keep their admirers *away* from them.

By and large, perception is reality; and when you're perceived as an expert, you have tremendous influence over the hearts and minds of your best prospects. That will drive people to seek you out and want do business with you. **Now you can build more profit margins into your products and services, and people will be more than happy to pay those premium prices,** because they have faith that they're dealing with an authority. This helps eliminate the emotional pain that comes from their marketplace confusion. By becoming an expert, you're not just helping yourself—you're helping your market, too!

This confusion is a growing trend, by the way. The marketplace will continue to become more saturated, and the average consumer will continue to face more and more choices on how to spend their money. This will cause more people to seek out experts.

So how do you become an expert? I've already told you that the decision to do so is the hardest part. Make that decision today. Convince yourself that you need to shift the balance of power in the marketing equation so people are chasing after you. **Once you've convinced yourself of this vital necessity, all you have to do is implement my third strategy to accomplish it.**

That strategy is to become an information marketer. Now, information marketing is a broad topic that covers many exciting subjects, and I only have enough room here to show you the tip of the iceberg. **But in every case, the process involves developing information-based products and services that**

provide a tangible value to your market. These can be books or reports, audio programs, seminars, workshops, DVD programs, consulting services, coaching programs—the ways you can deliver information are nearly endless, and there are many subtle variations. It's best to use a powerful combination of all these and more. For example, you can hold special events for your best clients, customers and prospects, teaching them the things they need to know the most.

Just don't get hung up on the format. I've been selling information since 1988, and the field changes constantly. It's honestly the most exciting, rewarding, challenging, and profitable kind of business to be in. Information marketing can be used in all kinds of traditional businesses to help attract and retain the very best prospective buyers. It's an easy format for establishing your credibility as an authority in your field—which you are, aren't you?

Here at M.O.R.E., Inc., we offer many different ways to help you cash-in on information marketing. We specialize in low-cost programs and opportunities, so you can get moving for a relatively small investment. Or if you prefer, you can Google "information marketing" on the Internet. I guarantee that you'll be amazed by the number of results. **This is a truly exciting and lucrative way to make money.** It can provide huge extra profits for your existing business, or it can become your main profit center.

Those are the three basic strategies you should use to get people to chase after you, and I hope you can see how well all three tie together. Now, let me give you a few stories of how other very smart marketers are using these strategies to attract prospects.

The first is a well-known marketing expert who claims he charges $5,000 an hour for one-on-one consulting. Now, I've known about him for decades now, and I've even paid him thousands of dollars over the years for his products; but I've never been willing to pay him $5,000 an hour or anywhere close to that, and I'm not sure anybody *really* has. I feel sorry for anyone who does; to me, that would be ridiculous! **And yet he claims to charge $5,000 an hour; and by doing so, he can take the position that he's the world's most expensive marketing consultant—which is not a bad position to find yourself in.**

When he has a seminar, he can charge people thousands of dollars to attend, because essentially he's positioned himself as somebody who's worth thousands of dollars an hour. If you're able to spend a few days with him (in a room filled with hundreds of other people!) you may feel you've received more than your money's worth, because you know his claims. He's also positioned himself as the marketing consultant who refuses to fly. So if you want to buy some of his time, you're going to have to fly to Los Angeles to meet with him—because he's not going to fly to you.

There are plenty of marketing consultants out there, and the irony is that many of them do a poor job of marketing and are struggling to survive. That seems odd and even funny to me, because here they are, claiming they can help people increase their sales and profits—and yet their own sales and profits are barely enough to keep them afloat. **This gentleman in LA doesn't have that problem; he's made millions of dollars and positioned himself as a real expert.** Of course, he's also developed hundreds of different products over the years: books, reports, and all kinds of recorded seminars that you can purchase for a fraction of his normal "$5,000/hour" fee.

He's got huge numbers of people chasing after him. That's why whenever he holds a seminar, hundreds of people pay thousands of dollars each to attend. **Is he really that much smarter than the rest of us? Probably not. He's smart enough to position himself as *the* expert in the field,** but he's definitely not worth that much when there are thousands of other marketing consultants who know just as much as or more than he does, and who will work very hard for you for a fraction of that price.

But again, perception is reality. When people discover (by reading his own sales literature!) that he charges $5,000 an hour, they think to themselves, "Jeez, he really must be worth it," and then they send away for one of his low-cost packages. Next they find out that they can attend a 2-3 day seminar where they can get *dozens* of hours of his expert time, and they flock to his seminars. He has a loyal following. **Whether he's smarter than all of the other marketing consultants or not, his most loyal clients swear by him and pay him a fortune.**

The next example comes from the late, great Gary C. Halbert, who was infamous for showing up at his own marketing seminars with hats and T-shirts that said "Clients Suck!" Think about how rude and offensive that is. People were paying thousands to attend his marketing seminars, only to be hit with that on arrival. But Gary could get away with it. **He was an obnoxious loose cannon—and all his loyal clients were convinced that he was a genius.** Well, we all know that we let people we think of as geniuses get away with things other people can't.

Authorities also have certain liberties the rest of us don't have (which is another reason why you should position yourself as an expert). Gary would get up in front of dozens or hundreds of people at his seminars wearing the message "Clients

Suck!", and proceed to tell them that he was *so* sick of helping all his clients make so much money, and how they never followed his advice even though he helped them make millions, and he had to fight them every step of the way. **He kept saying he was never going to take on another client again... so people worked very hard to convince him to take them on.**

The more he ranted and raved about all the millions of dollars that he made for people despite their refusal to follow his advice to the letter, the more people wanted to become his clients. **He did a marvelous job of positioning himself as a genuine expert and brilliant marketer — which he was.** Once people were convinced of that, they were willing to put up with his outrageous antics.

Another super-successful consultant started out as anything but. But back in his early days, when he was barely able to pay his bills, he'd routinely tell new prospects that his calendar was booked solid for weeks... even when it wasn't. **He was desperate for money, but he never, ever let that desperation show.** When he'd get someone on the phone who wanted to purchase his consulting services, he'd tell them, "Oh, I'm sorry. I'm booked up solid for the next three weeks straight. I might have an opening after that. Let me look... oh yes, I do have an opening on Tuesday the 27th at 3 PM. Will that work?" Even though it was all a marketing tactic, his prospects perceived that he was in high demand, and it made them want him even more.

One more example: there's a semi-famous copywriter who successfully promoted a very detailed information marketing course covering everything you have to know in order to create your own highly profitable ads and sales letters. He'd worked with some of the top consultants and other experts in the field, and had written copy for all their best clients, so he had a proven track record and a reputation as something of a whiz kid. Well, his program was huge—hundreds of pages thick—and included numerous audio recordings where he freely shared the tips, tricks and strategies he used.

At a cost of several hundred dollars, his information product was a steal, given all the time-tested secrets he shared. **So lots of people purchased it... and when they saw just how complicated it all was, many turned right around and paid him *thousands* of dollars to write ads and sales letters for them.** You may think that sounds ironic, but this fellow knew precisely what he was doing. He provided so much detail that it overwhelmed most people. It ended up being easier to hire him to use his methods than to try to emulate him.

Each of the preceding examples represents a case in which consultants combined Two Step Marketing and information marketing to position themselves as experts, in such a way as to get the very best prospects to chase after them. **But don't think that this will work only for people like them; these methods are universal, and can work in any type of business.** These strategies are limited only by your imagination.

Here's an example of a traditional business that uses this strategy to rake in huge profits. There's a gentleman on the West Coast who sells sheds and other small prefab buildings. You've seen companies like his in your area. People buy these structures because the quality of the construction is fairly high, while the prices can be quite low. So they're popular businesses, and he has a considerable amount of competition. But he's using the power of all three of the strategies I've outlined in this chapter to rise above his competitors and prove to buyers that they should choose his company over all the others. He'd had already been in business for a few years when he discovered the power of information marketing. He sent out several announcements to his customers, saying he was sponsoring a contest in which he would compile the best stories of how his customers were using his prefabricated buildings.

Because it was fun and creative, and because people wanted to win the contest, dozens wrote in about how happy they were with the building that they'd bought from his company, and how they were using it to save money instead of wasting it on storage fees, and in general discussed the creative ways they'd found to use his products to enhance their lives. **He compiled the stories into a nice little booklet that he then offered through Two-Step Marketing absolutely free, entitling it something like "57 Ways That My Small Buildings Can Help Improve Your Life."**

Because his customers were trying to win that contest, they put a lot of effort into those stories, and the stories oozed credibility. There were also pictures throughout the booklet of the structures that the customers had purchased, and of the customers themselves. He offered it absolutely free through radio ads, TV ads, and in the newspaper and direct mail, and it made him a fortune. **How? Because the people who took action to receive that booklet were already prime candidates for the products his company produced.** People loved reading the stories and looking at all the pictures, and it became an extremely powerful sales tool he used to convince people beyond any doubt that his company was the best choice. They then chased him because they felt his products could improve their lives, just like they had improved the lives of those 57 satisfied customers.

Those are just a few examples of how you can reverse the

power in the mercantile equation so that people chase you instead of you chasing them. The very best prospective buyers in your market *love* to buy things, and they're already searching for the benefits your products, services, and company offer—but they still hate to be sold. **They want to make the decision to seek you out, so the more you let them do that, the better off you are.** It doesn't matter that you made the first move; they could have ignored it. Instead, they sought you out. You never chased them. **This lets you charge more money for your products *and* make more sales faster. In the process, you'll build a loyal following who will continue to do business with you, and *only* you, for years.**

So think very deeply about the ideas I've outlined in this chapter, and begin to use this powerful strategy to reverse the power in the marketing relationship. Get all your best prospects and customers to chase after *you* instead of you chasing after *them*. **When you do that correctly, people will be happy to give you their disposable income.**

GOLDEN RULE SIXTEEN:

How to Develop Hot New Promotions That Drive People Crazy

There's an old saying that goes, "Quantity has a quality all its own." Indeed, in my experience, **quantity *leads* to quality. The secret to coming up with the best ideas is to come up with *lots* of ideas.** Go wild; don't hold back! Set a time every morning for brainstorming as many ideas as you can. Make it enjoyable to crank out huge quantities of ideas, and you'll be amazed at the little gems that emerge from this process.

Quantity leads to quality. Remember that. It's only four words, and it's catchy. **but it's also extremely wise, because implementing just a handful of well-executed ideas culled from your brainstorming sessions can make you rich.** I know this is true because I've done it, and I've seen other people do it. By getting into the habit of coming up with as many ideas as you can, you'll ultimately discover and develop strategies that can set you up financially for life. **With that in mind, here are some tips, tricks, and strategies you can use to develop ideas that have the power to make you enormous sums of money:**

1. Have fun.

2. Be creative.

3. See the idea-generating process as a challenging game.

4. Develop a group of brainstorming partners to help you create more ideas.

5. Get into the habit of coming up with as many ideas as you can.

6. Strive to master your marketplace.

Once you've come up with a slew of ideas, you then have to separate the very best from the rest. **And what *are* the best ideas? They're the ones that stand the greatest chance of making you the most money the fastest, for the longest period of time.** In order to come up with these winning ideas in your process of spinning ideas, you have to practice empathy—the most important characteristic of any marketer. **From a marketing context, empathy simply means developing a deeper understanding of the very best prospects in your market, considering things like:**

- Why do they buy what you sell?

- What they are looking for the most?

- What are their biggest fears, failures, and frustrations?

- What problems are keeping them up at night?

- What are their biggest unfulfilled desires?

- What items have they gone the craziest over in the past, and why?

- Why do your best customers keep doing business with

you?

- What are they looking for that they're not finding?

- What benefits excitement them the most?

- What are your most successful competitors doing right?

- What are your most successful competitors doing wrong?

- What ideas are working phenomenally well for others in your marketplace?

Here's my favorite question of all: If you had god-like superpowers and could give your prospects anything they wanted, what would it be, and how would you deliver it? That question unlocks your creativity part of your mind; and it's a truism that whenever you ask better questions, you get better answers. The key to coming up with a lot of good ideas is to constantly brainstorm, constantly drilling deeper and coming up with even more ideas.

The reason I love the "god-like superpowers" question is that you *don't* have god-like superpowers, and you know it—**yet by pretending you do, you can stretch the boundaries of what's possible.** Sometimes you come up with the wackiest answers... and often they're totally unworkable. But sometimes, those answers lead to breakthrough ideas that you might never have invented if you hadn't asked the question to begin with.

A great marketer is a cashflow artist; and it's ideas that start the money moving. This requires a lot of hard thinking, as you've probably figured out by now. But don't let that stop you. **If you can make it a game you play to win, then it**

becomes a labor of love. When you develop your first ideas that make the cash register ring, you'll be hooked for life. It's rewarding both emotionally and financially. **Keep asking yourself better questions, so you'll come up with better answers.** I guarantee that 95% of your competitors will never dig deeper than they already do; so when you do, you'll end up light years ahead of them.

When that happens, a lot of the money they'd otherwise earn will go to you. Doesn't that excite you? I hope so! Having an abundance of money might not make you happy, but it'll usually make you smile. It's something you can get passionate about, and it's something that will put the joy back in your business. Therefore, I encourage you to try it.

Here's a simple brainstorming process you can use to make the game even more exciting and profitable. First, spend a few days answering the questions on the list I outlined a few pages back. **Write down everything you can think of; your goal is to create the longest list possible.** Don't worry about duplicating items. When you can't add another thing, start editing the list. You'll end up with a list of assumptions about your marketplace that becomes one column of a three-column chart. **The next column lists products and services you can offer your prospects that address those assumptions.** For example: one of my assumptions is that my customers hate buying something and then not having any contact with my company after the purchase. They want us to stay in touch, and want to know what we're doing to help them further. Many of my competitors just disappear after the sale, and the customers feel used, manipulated, and cheated. **We strive to create follow-up services that help us keep in touch with our customers after the sale, to prove they made the right decision to purchase from us.** We also undertake other relationship-building activities to help them suffer less from buyer's remorse, and realize that we really are different from the competitors who take their money and run.

In the third column, include any ideas you can think of that are counter to the assumption, or any special problems or challenges you have with that assumption. Let's go back to the assumption that our customers are reluctant to buy things from us because they assume we won't stay in touch with them. This can cause buyer's remorse and make them question their decision. In Column 2 (the product/service ideas column), we create specific solutions that make it easy for us to stay in touch with them and help them realize that they made the right decision by purchasing our product or service. We also remind them of what we're doing to give them more of what they want. **In Column 3, we might record things something like how expensive it is to stay in touch with our customers, and how we're trying to limit our fixed overhead.**

By the way, we prefer to use the word "challenge" instead of "problem." According to a definition I've got hanging on my wall, a challenge is "difficulty in a job that is stimulating to the one engaged in it." It's hard, but that's why you love it. **Most people perceive problems as things to run away from— whereas they run *toward* challenges. So try to reframe all your problems as challenges.** The reason why the third column is so important is because, just like the first two columns, it's a tool that helps you come up with ideas that you might never have considered otherwise.

This three-column chart is a simple way for you to develop your most creative breakthroughs, and point the way toward products and services that the people in your market

will go crazy over. It's a tool that lets you do your very best thinking, so consider using it to quickly find and develop your very best ideas—the ones that get more people to gladly give you more money on a regular basis.

Your Company's Most Important Hidden Asset

If you've been in business for any time at all, you possess a certain hidden asset that can make you rich. The best thing is, this hidden asset is also hidden from all your competitors. Once you understand and take advantage of its true value, you'll enjoy an instant and unfair advantage in your marketplace. **The secret is simply this: your mailing list is everything.** The more promotions you run to your existing customers, and the better your relationship with them is, the more value will accrue to your mailing list.

America's first billionaire, Andrew Carnegie, once said: "You can take away all my factories, all my machinery, all my equipment, all of my real estate, and leave me with my very best people—and I'll have it all back in no time flat." I love that quote, because I firmly believe in the value of good people. However, I want to add one more distinction. I say: "Take away everything from me, but leave me my best people *and my mailing list* and I'll have it all back in no time flat." **That's because a good mailing list is your meal ticket for life. It can produce enormous lifetime sales and profits.**

It's so much easier to sell to your existing customers than it is to sell to people who've never done business with you before. Your existing customers already know that you deliver. So the first key to implementing this strategy is to understand just how valuable your mailing list is. It's everything. **Keep**

**developing new products and services that give them more of
what they want the most—and keep building your mailing list.**

I'm shocked at the number of small businesses that *don't*
stay in touch with their best customers on a regular basis.
What shocks me even more are all the small businesses that are
constantly chasing after new customers and paying very little
attention to their existing customers. Their attitude is that their
existing customers know where they are, and when they need
more of what they sell, they'll come back automatically. **That's a
huge mistake... because you can't be sure it will happen.**

Think of the best restaurant you've ever visited. If you're
like me, you probably frequent several restaurants that have been
very successful for years—even decades. I love using this
restaurant analogy, because everyone has a favorite restaurant or
two; and it's easy to see that the secret to having a profitable
restaurant is getting the customers to return repeatedly. Once they
become loyal customers, they tell their friends and family,
generating even more business. That's the secret of success for
every restaurant.

But that's also the secret of success for *every* business. **No
matter what business you're in, getting customers to come
back and do business with you repeatedly, for as long as
possible, is the key to success.** In order to do that you have to
invite them to come back and do more business with you. You
can't just wait for them to come to you. It's easy enough to be
proactive. All you have to do is keep your mailing list in some
type of a spreadsheet or similar program, then contact those
people on a regular basis. **Develop new products, services, and
offers that give them more of what you know is most
important to them. Show them you really do care.** Every

---

business claims they care about their customers, but what are you doing to prove it?

That's how most of your customers feel: *what have you done for me lately?* Just like the Janet Jackson song from the 1990s. So stay in touch with them, make them additional offers, hold special events just for them, and inform them of items you think might be of interest to them. **It's all about relationship building.** The first key to building a good relationship is to show people you really care about them. That can be very easy to do if you have the systems and processes in place that let you do it.

Once you've put your mailing list into a spreadsheet program, **segment that list by separating out your best customers. You define the best customers based on the amount of money they've spent with you.** People tell you how serious they are by the actions they take. That's why those who spend the most money should immediately be separated from the rest of your customers.

Then constantly think of new things you can do specifically for them, to catch and hold their interest, and use direct mail to stay in touch with them. You can also have someone call them on the telephone, or use social media to solidify those bonds. Do all you can to make them feel important and special, and keep offering them new products and services you feel they'll be interested in. *Customers go where they're invited and stay where they're appreciated.* Remember that! Write it down and burn it into your brain.

If doing all this was simple and easy, then everybody would be doing it—and you know they're not. Most businesses aren't paying close enough attention to their old customers, because at

---

first glance it seems easier to chase new customers than to put energy into solidifying existing relationships. **Yet when their old customers see those "new customers only" promotions, they become resentful.** They start thinking, "What am I, a walking wallet? I should be getting a special offer too. You should be doing something special for *me*. What have you done for me lately?"

Some business people *can* see the obvious, though, and many of them ask me, "What can I offer my existing customers?" The answer is something of a riddle: you offer them the same things, only different. **Here's what I mean: you want to give them more of what they bought in the past, but with unique twists.** The new items have to be similar enough that they provide the same basic benefits and advantages that caused your customers to buy in the first place, but they must be unique enough that your existing customers get excited all over again.

If something is too new, many people will be put off and hold back because of fear. But if it's too similar to what you're selling, they'll say to themselves, "I've seen this before," and they'll be bored and apathetic. Bored people don't buy.

So there's your riddle—and you can spend years trying to invent ways to solve it. In fact, **you should, because making additional offers to existing customers is the fastest, simplest, and above all *easiest* way to get more people to give you more money.** I find it shocking that a company's mailing list almost never shows up on their assets list; that's why I call it a "hidden" asset. Despite that, **it's THE most important asset you have.**

Build and maintain strong relationships with people who have done business with you before. Make it easy for them to keep doing business with you, and you'll leave your competitors eating your dust. It's as simple as that.

GOLDEN RULE EIGHTEEN:

A Gentle Reminder

One of the smartest things you can do is work through other people. **Find as many capable, competent, trustworthy people you can, integrate them into your team, delegate to them, and train them to run the day-to-day part of your business.** That way, you can focus on the areas that make you the most profits. Do this. You'll work less and make more money.

Too many business people are trying to wear all the hats at once, so they do a lousy job of delegating. They believe that hiring the best people is something that costs them money, never **thinking that that's not, in fact, the case. The best people make you far more money than they cost.** As long as have the right systems and processes in place and manage them properly, you can transform your business into a virtual ATM that cranks out more money even as you personally work less.

This is the lazy person's secret to getting rich—and it's something you can implement in your business starting right now.

The #1 Thing Your Prospects Are Starving For... and Aren't Getting

The people in your marketplace are absolutely starving for a little genuine recognition. That sounds simple enough, but don't let that simplicity fool you; **this is *very* important.** We're living in an age when we're all busier than ever, and most of us feel unappreciated—especially when it comes to the companies that want our money. In this overcrowded, over-hyped marketplace, companies that make us feel special will always get our money first. **It's easiest to win people's money when you win their hearts first.**

So how do you win their hearts? Gain their trust and make them feel important. Pretend everyone you meet has a huge sign on his or her forehead flashing, "Make me feel important!" over and over. Try this just for fun; and then realize that your job as a marketer is to do just what the sign says. **The people who give you money on a regular basis (or the prospects you want to chase after you) are crucial.** Without them, you wouldn't have a business. So your job is to make them feel as special as you possibly can.

Now, when it comes to spending money, people are extremely selfish. **They think only about themselves and what you can do for them**—and no wonder. These days, they're inundated with so many different possibilities for spending their money. **This is why they'll always give more money to the**

companies that make them feel special and appreciated. This simple idea works in business-to-business marketing and consumer marketing both, and it's responsible for billions of dollars worth of annual sales.

My wife Eileen and I started our direct response marketing business in September 1988. Thanks to the help, support, and guidance of marketing consultants like Russ von Hoelscher, we quickly generated millions of dollars. Our success made us hungry to learn everything we could about direct response marketing, to the point that we became obsessed with it. So we hired a bunch of direct marketing consultants and paid them a fortune to teach us their tips, tricks, and strategies. **Several of those consultants did a powerful job of winning our hearts by making us feel very special.** They went out of their way to invite us to private, client-only events, and asked us to participate in special meetings consisting of small groups of their most elite clients.

Those are the consultants that we gave the most of our money to. **We paid over $100,000 to one famous direct-response marketing consultant, in fact, because he did the most effective job of making us feel appreciated.** We joined his small group of elite clients; and because he's world-famous, we felt privileged to do so. We learned a great deal from him, but we gave him a small fortune in the process.

Looking back, I can easily see that although this fellow is truly a brilliant marketer and great teacher, at least a half-dozen other marketing consultants we hired over the years were just as good as he was—**yet we didn't give them our money, because they had no plan for doing special things that made us feel valued, and important.** *That's* what people want more than anything else. The good news is that there are plenty of things you can do to make your best customers feel this way.

One of the small businesses I work with is the pet boutique that my wife owns. Eileen does a wonderful job of marketing her business. She hosts all kinds of special events for her customers—an average of three per month. When she does, she takes lots of pictures and puts them up on Facebook. She tells stories about her best customers, and posts the very best pictures on a bulletin board in the store. **She makes her customers feel appreciated, applying that simple process to all the events she hosts.**

This is something you can also do. Even if some of your best clients or customers never attend your events, at least they'll feel appreciated when you repeatedly send them those invitations. **This separates you from all your competitors, because they can "feel the love"—and they'll reciprocate by doing more business with you.**

Write down this question: "What can I do this month to make a small group of my best customers or clients feel special, valued, and appreciated?" Read it, reread it, and think about it. You don't have to come up with an answer immediately; just write the question down and contemplate it, and let the answers start coming to you. **Make this your focus, because remember: the fastest, simplest, and easiest way to make extra profits in your business is to get your best customers to do more business with you.**

Instead of putting all your resources into chasing after new clients, **put 70-80% of your marketing dollars, time, and effort into the various ways you can make your best clients**

feel appreciated. You can do all kinds of things that they perceive are just for them, from limited sales to new product development to special events—**and they'll respond by giving you more of their money.**

GOLDEN RULE TWENTY:

Why You Should NEVER Sell By Price

You've probably seen hundreds of businesses claim to offer the lowest prices in their marketplaces. Well, maybe they do—but for most marketers, even making the claim is a huge mistake. **People who focus on price will never be loyal to you, because the money is all they care about.** They'll jump from supplier to supplier, the way hookers jump from bed to bed. You may hate that analogy, but I believe it's something you'll never forget—which is why I used it. It may not be PC, but it's accurate and memorable!

Price buyers just aren't loyal, and you're looking for loyal customers who will stay with you for the longest possible time and spend the maximum amount of money.

One of my best business friends is my printer, Steve Harshbarger. I've given Steve millions of dollars worth of printing business for almost 20 years, because he's an extremely honest man and I trust him. **He'll go out of his way to do everything possible to serve his clients in every way he can.** If I had a huge problem at three o'clock in the morning, I have a very small list of people that I would call for help—and Steve is on that list. He's become a friend as well as one of my most important suppliers.

Steve earned my trust when I first met him, because he

told me the truth about my concerns. He didn't BS me, and that really woke me up. I was used to salespeople who told me what they thought I wanted to hear; but when I asked Steve if he offered the lowest prices in the business back in the early 1990s, he said, "Sometimes yes, sometimes no." Then he explained to me why that was.

If it was the kind of job that worked best on his equipment, he told me, he could definitely give me the best price; but if it was something that wouldn't be economical on his equipment, then I could get a better price elsewhere. He just flat-out told me, **"Remember, T.J., you can have any one or maybe two of three things: the best price, the highest quality, or the fastest service. But you can never have all three."** I never forgot that, and you shouldn't either. That was a valuable lesson; it woke me up like a cold slap of truth. **He's been getting my business ever since then.**

Now, low prices are important to your best customers too; but **what people are really searching for is the highest value for the lowest price.** So it's up to you to do all you can to educate them on why your products and services are worth far more money than you're asking them for in return. **Do all you can to build as much value into your products and services as possible.** You can't do that and be the low-cost provider.

I started my first business, a carpet and upholstery cleaning company, in December 1985. I was dead broke at the time, and literally homeless. I had just broken up with a young woman I was living with, and had moved out of her house. I was sleeping on the couches and floors of a handful of my friends. Otherwise, I was living out of the backseat of my car. I was cleaning carpets at the time to get by, and then a friend of mine said, "Hey, T.J., let's start our own carpet cleaning business!"

Even though he was dead broke, just like I was, we did it. And because we were so poor, our equipment was in terrible shape. The van we bought for $1,000 (by putting $100 down and paying $100 a week until it was paid off) was a wreck. **The only way we knew to get jobs was to offer super-low prices.** Over the next few months, we knocked on thousands of doors and practically begged people to let us come clean their carpets and upholstery for next to nothing. Our entire marketing strategy was built around doing the job for the lowest possible price.

We attracted quite a few customers, and slowly built up a reputation thanks to word-of-mouth and the fact that we did high-quality work. Yet, because we *were* charging such low prices, we never had enough money to buy better equipment or do the more expensive kinds of marketing that would have been more effective. **We were prisoners of our low pricing strategies.**

Although we did develop a lot of great customers who had us back repeatedly to clean their carpets and upholstery, there were many prospects who took one look at our beat-up van and equipment (and us!) and said, "No thank you." **We were turned away by many more people than we actually attracted because we were the lowest-cost provider, and people equate low prices with things that are cheap and tawdry.** People don't want cheap, tawdry things; **what they want are valuable things for dirt-cheap prices.** That's not just a play on words; there's a genuine difference there. So when I say price buyers are like hookers, please understand that it's only a metaphor!

All of my very best clients for my first business were wonderful people, and we gave them top-notch work; but **we**

never had enough profits to build the business. We were stuck with being that low-cost provider, which is one reason to avoid the strategy. Another reason to avoid it is that eventually, someone will come along and offer even lower prices than you—and then, if you want to compete with them, you start a race to the bottom. Either way, it's a zero-sum game. You never have enough profits to build your business as it could and should be built. In order to do that, **you have to charge premium prices. Along with these premium prices, you have to deliver premium services**—and you have to educate your customers in every way as to why the extra money you're asking them to give you is worth it.

Now, fast-forward two decades. My current company is a premium-priced provider. Out of our thousands of competitors from coast-to-coast, we charge some of the highest prices in the industry. **In order to start doing that, we had to break out of our comfort zone.** It was very uncomfortable at first to charge five or ten times more money than our competitors were charging. **Yet, we took that risk—and once we broke through and made the transition, we made more money than we'd ever made before.**

We've discovered some major advantages along the way. **First, when you charge higher prices, you get higher quality customers.** The people who spend the most money with you will give you the fewest customer service hassles, and tend to be delightful people to do business with. You should charge more money for that reason alone: you'll attract a better quality of customer. **Also, you require fewer sales to make more profits.** In other words, you can make big profits from bad numbers. What do I mean by that? Simply this: when the majority of your products and services sell for small amounts of money and razor-thin profits, then you need a high percentage of response to make any money. **Conversely, higher ticket items mean that you require fewer responses to profit.**

This also means you'll need fewer customers to make those profits. **You can serve those fewer customers in a much better way than if you were a low-cost provider and were forced to serve a larger number of customers.**

Charging higher prices *is* **a risk.** I'll never forget how scared we were when we held our first $5,000 seminar in 1996. Prior to that we'd done over three dozen low-cost seminars; so we went from charging hundreds of dollars to charging several thousand. It was frightening, and yet we took the plunge. We surrounded ourselves with a team of great joint venture business partners who helped us pull off that event, and we focused tightly on the audience. **We did everything possible to make their experience truly life-changing.** Our goal was to make it so that at the end of the event they said, "Wow! That was worth far more than $5,000." **We channeled all our fear and insecurities into doing everything possible to give the customer the most valuable experience we possibly could.**

That's another thing the extra profits you generate when you charge premium prices allow you to do. **They give you the freedom and flexibility to serve your customers at a higher level, which you just can't do when you're selling for low prices.**

So: never aim for the low price. If you must focus on price, utilize premium pricing instead. Use this secret well, and you'll end up with a smaller, more select group of customers who will spend large amounts of money with you over long periods of time, making you the envy of your competitors.

GOLDEN RULE TWENTY ONE:

How to Make Money Over and Over on the Same Promotions

As you know, the big secret to making massive profits is to get your best customers to buy from you as often as possible for the maximum profit per transaction. Do that with a large enough group and you'll get rich. It's that simple. **Reselling to your existing customers is key to maximum profitability.**

As I've emphasized more than once in this book, the best way to do that is to just keep giving your customers the same stuff you gave them before, but with a new twist added each time. **If your products and services are perceived as old hat, your customers will be bored—and bored people never buy. Whatever's current creates currency.**

On the other hand, if a product or service is too new and different, they won't buy then, either. Many will be afraid to do so. **Therefore, you have to deliver products and services that** *seem* **innovative and exciting, but nonetheless contain familiar themes your customers are already comfortable with.** If you're selling ketchup, don't suddenly try to sell them mustard. Sell them a new variety of ketchup. Even then, don't make it too different! A slightly spicier red ketchup will sell better than even the tastiest green or purple ketchup (this has been proven). What you need, then, is basically old wine in new bottles. Most people are searching for variations on a theme, not a completely new theme.

They proved their interest by giving you their money in the first place. **People vote with their pocketbooks,** so take a close look at the products, services and promotions that have worked the very best for you, and realize that somewhere within those items are the things that your best customers (and prospects just like them) value the most. It's up to you to determine what those common denominators are, and then to add those to the items you develop in the future.

The newness will attract your customer's attention, while the old and familiar will hold that attention by making them feel comfortable with your new offers. When you learn how to apply this secret properly, you can keep offering your best clients and customers the same basic types of products and services again and again—which means all the prep work is easier. **You can reuse a lot of the same sales material, simply tailoring it to the new offerings.** You gain enormous leverage because your "new" products and services are really your "old" products and services with new twists.

Here's a real-world example: the most recent Ford Mustangs (as of 2012) look a great deal like the original Mustangs from the mid-to-late 1960s. In the '70s and '80s they changed the model a little too much—they got away from the familiar, and their sales took a hit. Now the newer models resemble the original models again, though with a modern look and feel. That's a great example of giving people things they're familiar with while modifying them enough for the new to show.

One of our most successful recent promotions here at M.O.R.E., Inc. has been a series of advertising and management services. We're on our ninth edition of this promotion—and it's simply a riff on best of the best of everything we've developed for the previous versions. **All the hard work, thousands of person-hours of time, has already been invested; now we're reaping the harvest with the ninth version.** It required *some* investment of time and effort, but not nearly as much as the previous editions. It looks and feels different from the previous versions, but it's essentially the same service with a few great additions.

Think of this as the marketing principle of evolution. You're constantly looking for ways to make your best products and services appear new, different, and special, so you keep tweaking them, constantly adding new elements. That way, you can keep using the sales materials you've used in the past, with slight (but vital) modifications to make them look and feel different.

On the other hand, when you do find a revolutionary product or service that's totally different from anything else in the marketplace, that doesn't mean you have to ignore it. Just inject a familiar element, or compare it with something people in your marketplace are already familiar with. **Right now, we're promoting a revolutionary new healthcare service called *telemedicine*.** This is a concierge service that gives people direct access to a team of medical doctors in their own state who are on call 24 hours a day to help them with their medical needs. For as little as pennies a day, tens of millions of people can now pick up their cell phones and get direct access to a team of board-certified medical doctors. **This is a service that we believe will revolutionize the healthcare industry — and generate billions of dollars in pure profits every month.**

The brilliant company that developed this breakthrough is using the power of network marketing to reward average people who introduce their service to prime prospects. **Because it's brand-new, this opportunity offers real consumer excitement.**

The millions of people in the business opportunity market that we serve are *always* looking for something new and exciting—but again, if it's unproven they get scared, and like bored people, scared people don't buy. **Therefore, we have to prove to them that although this idea is revolutionary, it still incorporates ingredients that have already been proven profitable.**

We do this by comparing the telemedicine concierge service with the concept of prepaid legal services, which hit the market in 1983. Prepaid legal services, which provide customers direct access to a team of legal advisers for a monthly fee, use a very similar business model—one that's made thousands of distributers wealthy. **That's all the proof our clients require for them to see that telemedicine has the potential to make them all the money they'll ever want or need.** Even though telemedicine is a completely different field, the phenomenal success story of prepaid legal services—which are delivered in a similar way— helps to educate and persuade our prospects. In fact, telemedicine might even prove more profitable than prepaid legal services. **Most of us need access to a lawyer just a few times in our lives, but you might need medical help at any time—and healthcare is much more important to most of us than legal aid.**

That makes it easier to sell this revolutionary offer. **We've wrapped it around something that already has a rock-solid track record.** This helps to ease the prospect's concerns, making them feel comfortable with the service, despite the fact that it's entirely new. **So: when developing new products to offer to your clients, think about all the ways you can prove them similar to things your clients are already comfortable with right now.**

Keep giving them more of what you know they want the most, and you'll make more money with less work.

How to Get the Best Prospects to Start Giving You More Money Right Now

This one secret alone can move you into the top position in your marketplace, and thereby change the way you've always thought about your business.

Here's the secret: **You must position yourself as the top expert in your market.** I've already talked about this necessity as part of a three-part marketing plan in an earlier chapter, but this is one of those strategies I just can't overemphasize. Given the choice, people prefer to give their money to an expert, so why not become one? That should be reason enough, but here are some other reasons you should never hesitate to blow your own horn. First of all, nobody's going to do it for you (unless you pay them to). **This means that you have to sell yourself before you sell your product or service. In order to sell yourself, you must position yourself as an expert.**

Second, the average consumer has more choices today than ever before. They're confused and frustrated by the endless decisions they're faced with regarding whom to do business with. All those people are yelling at them to try their products and services, so naturally, **when faced with a new buying decision, they'll look for the best qualified, most knowledgeable experts they can find** — and will always give their business to those people first. That's why *you* have to be one of those people.

Many of your prospects are extremely fearful, skeptical, and cynical. They're afraid of making the wrong decision, of losing their money. **The thing that people want the most is *certainty* — the feeling that everything's going to be okay, that they'll get precisely what they were promised in exchange for their cash.** When they perceive you as an expert, they have a higher degree of certainty and will give you their money faster.

This is an excellent way to separate yourself from all your competitors. An expert has the authority that people are looking for; most of us respond very well to authority figures. We're trained to do so since birth. So declare yourself an expert. When enough people are convinced that you *are* an expert, then other people who have little or nothing to gain financially will declare you an expert too. But it all starts with you.

In a bit, I'll give you a few simple strategies you can use to immediately position yourself as the expert in your field; but first, I'm going to let you in on the #1 reason why more small business people don't do this. Just as we're conditioned from a very young age to listen to authority, we're conditioned not to talk too highly of ourselves. **We're trained to never stick our necks out or pat ourselves on the back.** Otherwise, people call us vain, egotistical, braggarts, showoffs. It's extremely painful for most people to even begin to declare themselves experts, because they feel phony doing so.

However, the fact is that any time you know more about a particular topic than your prospects (especially in regard to the products and services you sell) then you *are* an expert. That's one of the things we've always told our sales representatives here at M.O.R.E, Inc. If you just study our sales materials, then you'll know much more than most of the prospects, because they *won't* take the time to study them.

The first step toward declaring yourself as an expert is to convince yourself that you *are* an expert. If you feel like you're being fake or phony, then spend a significant amount of time studying not just your products and services, but your market in general. You'll soon gain tremendous confidence on the subject. **The second step is to stick your neck out, overcoming the social conditioning that demands you do otherwise.** Learn to do so for the sake of the business. People want to do business with experts, so give them what they want.

Your competitors, whether they're consciously doing so or not, are making every effort to assure your shared prospects that they can deliver all the results and promises they claim for their line of products and services. You must do the same for your own line. **A major part of selling is a transference of belief and emotion;** in other words, the more convinced you are that you're an expert and the more you express confidence in yourself, then the more confidence other people will have in you. They'll be less hesitant about giving you their money.

It's easier to do this than you might imagine, and it's a lot of fun. My favorite method is to develop information products. If you Google "information marketing" on the 'Net, you'll find a wealth of information about this powerful form of selling. **Developing information products is exciting, it's creative, it's challenging, it's rewarding, and it's *extremely* profitable.** Information products can encompass a wide variety of print, audio, video, and Internet-based products and services.

Developing an information product is as easy as grabbing a dirt-cheap digital recorder or even an old-fashioned audiocassette recorder, jotting down a handful of notes about the main benefits and features of your product or service, and then speaking freely into the recorder. **Do your very best job of explaining all the reasons why what you're offering gives people much more value than the amount of money you're asking for in exchange, and why you have all of the qualifications to help them**—*and* why you and your company can help them better than anyone else trying to get their business. Just talk.

Those recordings can be given away to prospects as a way of generating leads, or they can be sold for a small amount to people who want and need the main benefits you can provide them. If your recordings lack power or you're self-conscious about them, then simply have them transcribed, and give the printed transcripts to a writer who can edit them, smooth out the writing, and make it easier to read. **You can write, you can record, you can get in front of a video camera, or you can go in front of a live event.** Whatever you do, teach your prospects why the items you offer are worth far more in terms of real-world benefits than the money you're asking them to give you in exchange.

Your information products educate people on why you, your company, or your products and services are the best choice. They help establish you as the most credible authority. They help you build a relationship with your best prospects and customers. They can be icebreakers, letting people get to know you a little bit better—which is the first stage in getting people to like and trust you.

You can develop an almost endless variety of information products to use as part of your overall marketing process. If you're a writer, start writing. If you're a better speaker, start speaking. Again, there are plenty of talented writers who can turn your recording transcripts into readable information products. Other specialists can take the audio you record and edit out the bad areas so people only hear the parts where you're speaking in the most authoritative, powerful way. That can be done with video, too. Finally, there's also a tremendous energy to be found in live events. Partly this is because you're taking all of the focus off yourself and putting it onto your prospects

The more of these information products you develop, the more of an expert you'll become. And it's easy — highly addicting, even. That's why I've developed hundreds of different audio and video products, and why we've done hundreds of events of all kinds. It's why I've published so many books and reports. I just love it! **It's such a creative way to make money, because when you're 100% focused on giving your prospects the greatest information you possibly can, providing them all the benefits that are most important to them, then you really are serving them in the highest possible way.** You're not just writing, recording, and filming yourself so that you can show off how great you are. It's the exact opposite of being egotistical, because your entire focus is on helping others.

Educate your prospects and customers on all the reasons why they should be giving you more of their money on a regular basis, and solidify those relationships so they'll continue to do so. **If you do it right, they'll come to you presold, ready to give you even more of their money right away, with the least amount of sales resistance.** When you're actively involved in information marketing, and keep developing a wide range of products, services and events designed to convince, persuade, and educate, then the very best buyers in your market will seek you out. **This is the**

ultimate sales resistance breaker, even for new buyers.

You already know that the secret to getting rich in your business is to get more people to do more business with you, for more profit, more often, with greater efficiency. There's no better strategy for that than information marketing. Get on the Internet and do your due diligence. **Learn everything you can about this powerful form of salesmanship, start creating your first information products, and you'll quickly move into the top position in your marketplace.**

GOLDEN RULE TWENTY THREE:

Spot and Exploit the Hidden Gaps in Your Market

What is a gap in the marketplace? It's a need or desire that's not being properly fulfilled. Every market has gaps, but you'll only find them through relentless searching. Once you do discover a powerful need or desire, fill it in a different and better way than your competition's doing—if they're filling it at all. **Either way, start hammering wedges into the gap, and you'll have a huge competitive advantage.**

You have to start by asking yourself, "What are the best prospects in my marketplace really searching for? What benefits are most important to them? Why do they buy the products or services we sell? What's the biggest emotional reason? What is the driving force behind their repeat purchases? What are the needs and desires that are not being fulfilled, and how can we fill them in the most powerful and profitable way?" **Questions like that will lead to preliminary answers, which will lead, in turn, to better questions and better answers.**

One reason why there are hidden gaps in your market is because many of your competitors are simply following the follower. **They're all doing the same things. Nobody is really standing out by doing something bold or different. Another reason is simply because you and your competitors aren't thinking deeply enough about all this.** You're looking at surface answers instead of the *real* answers. You have to realize that the best answers to your questions will evolve over a period of time. The more you think about them, the better your answers will be.

So get behind your prospect's eyeballs. *Become* **them.** Talk to as many of them as you possibly can, asking them frankly about what they're searching for the most. What competitors are they buying from now? What products or services have they liked the most in the past? Which ones have they disliked or hated? Which of your competitors do the best jobs, and which ones do the worse?

If you ask enough of your prospects and customers these questions over a long enough period of time, you're going to see common denominators, and skate right past the surface answers. That's where people usually stop; they never dig deeper, never thinking about this in a prolonged way. They stop asking themselves these questions—and they shouldn't. You can't find gaps in the marketplace if you stop searching for them. **Keep digging for those gold nuggets that people want and respond to the most, the things that get them the most excited, so that they'll stand in line with money in hand and practically beg you to take it.** That's the power of finding and exploiting these gaps.

In addition to getting to know your customers better, gather as much information as possible on your competitors. Which are the ones to beat? Who's making the best sales and profits? What are they doing right—and conversely, what are they doing wrong? How can you take advantage of both? Those are questions that sometimes take years to answer, because they require a thorough study of the marketplace.

In order to do that, you have to step back and look at the big picture. You can't be caught up in the day-to-day part of your business *and* answer those really deep questions effectively. **If**

you're too involved in working in your business, you're too close to the forest to see through the trees. You have to let other people run the day-to-day affairs—and then you have to grill those people relentlessly. Because they're involved on the front lines, they have direct contact and communication with your best clients and customers, and they know things that they don't even *know* they know.

You have to brainstorm with your best staff members on a regular basis to dig deeper inside the heads and hearts of your best customers. Doing this helps you develop an intimate understanding of exactly what those people are searching for the most, so you can develop products or services that fulfill those emotional needs and desires. **This will better serve them, whereupon you can begin attracting more people who are just like them but haven't done business with you yet.**

Reaching this point may require years of commitment and dedication to understanding the hearts and minds of the people you sell to. Who are they, and what are their greatest commonalities? What are they searching for the most? What causes them to re-buy the kind of products or services you sell? What do they love? What do they hate? What are their biggest fears, failures, and frustrations? What are their biggest problems and challenges? What solutions and results are they searching for the most? What's most important to them, above everything else, in relationship to what you sell? **Those are questions that need to keep playing in your brain like an endless loop recording.**

So make it your mission to uncover the hidden gaps in the marketplace, and then pry them open in ways that your competitors haven't. **When you make that a primary focus, you'll have a huge advantage over your competitors.**

GOLDEN RULE TWENTY FOUR:

The Alchemical Connection

Copywriters are true alchemists. **We transform ordinary paper, ink, and digital information into something worth far more than gold. We create actual *wealth*.** We will it into existence with our knowledge and skill. We suck the money out of the marketplace and into our bank accounts. Does that sound exciting? I hope so! Visualize it. See it. That *should* excite you.

If your marketplace is big enough, there are millions or even tens or hundreds of millions of dollars out there waiting for you right now. All you have to do is find a way to convince a small percentage of the millions of people in your market that the products or services you're offering are worth far more than the money you're asking for them to give you in exchange. Again, it's not easy—but it *is* simple, so whenever you get frustrated or confused, just remember that.

If you start with a big enough group of people who have a strong enough desire for the types of products and services you sell, and if what you're offering them can give them more of what they're searching for the most, *and* you can find a way to do it profitably, then the question is not, "Will I get rich?" the only question is "How rich will I get, and how long will it take me?" **You philosopher's stone is copywriting: good, honest direct response copywriting where the words you write (or otherwise communicate to your audience) fan the fires of their desires, exciting them enough to give you more of their money.** This is a skill that you can develop, given sufficient time and practice.

If you remember your history lessons in school, the original alchemists back in the Middle Ages were looking for a way to turn lead into gold. Little did they know that the only way to do that is in a nuclear reactor! The early alchemists were actually the first chemists. Well, as a direct response marketing copywriter, you're doing something similar, except your "base materials" are paper, ink, and imagination. **Words are power—in fact, they're the only magic you'll ever be able to tap into in this lifetime.**

Study everything about copywriting that you possibly can. **Make a decision that you're going to develop this skill—and realize above all that this *is* a skill, and that you can learn it.** The very best copywriters have the ability to write a profitable sales letter in as little as a few days. **Imagine that kind of power.** Imagine being able to inspire thousands of people to pull out their credit cards and authorize you to charge whatever amount of money you're asking for, because they read your copy and they're convinced they can't live without your product or service.

That's the power that the world's greatest DRM copywriters wield. The words we write, or dictate into a recording machine, or that we speak on an audio or visual presentation, have a fantastic ability to influence the people within our marketplace to transfer money from their bank accounts into ours.

This is a skill that can make you rich, which means it's worth learning how to do. It may take you a lot of time and sacrifice to truly master the skill, but it's worth all the time and effort—because once you've mastered it, it can make you a millionaire in no time flat. **I say that with the voice of authority, because it's done exactly that for me.**

Take Enormous Risks – and Play It Safe at the Same Time

With this Golden Rule, you can lose money on nine out of ten of your new ideas—and still end up making a fortune. The secret is to test everything first, carefully but aggressively. All it takes is one winner every once in a while to not only recoup your losses on the items that didn't pan out, but also to run up profits in the millions. Again, I know this is true because it's one of the ways I've built my own fortune.

Let me make it very clear from the beginning that *you will never find your greatest winners without aggressive testing*. That's all there is to it, unless you just stumble onto something special—and since when is marketing a lottery? Even if you do stumble onto something profitable, you're going to need to know how to follow it up successfully, or you're just another one-hit wonder.

Thanks to the power of direct response marketing, you can test your most aggressive ideas for products, services, and promotions for very small sums. Think of yourself as a wildcatter oilman drilling wells wherever your research takes you. Inevitably, most will be dry holes. But all it takes is one strike to pay for all the failures—and then some. Same here. If you test very carefully, inexpensively sampling your marketplace before you roll something out big-time, you're never going to lose it all on one roll of the dice. **But once you've found**

something and proven it does work, if your marketplace is big enough, you could potentially make millions once you roll your promotion out in a big, bold way.

So many people are worried about losing money that they never take the risks necessary to *make* money. With this principle, you have to set out with a willingness to lose money, which is alien to those people's mindset. Your goal is to try all kinds of combinations of your best ideas as fast as possible for a low cost each time. **It's quick, dirty, and cheap.** Then you study the numbers to see if any of those tests proved out, at least well enough that you can make a decent profit when you do roll it out.

Just start with the very best plans you have, and think them through in the deepest possible way before you begin testing. **The very best plans are those combinations of products, services, and promotions that have made you the most money in the past, or which have worked the best for other people.** Once you've made those plans, make small, aggressive tests of what you perceive as the best variants of these plans. Use your biggest, boldest tactics, the ones you're the most afraid of. If something doesn't scare you a little, you probably shouldn't do it. **It's got to be revolutionary, and you have to be willing to spend money to make money.**

You don't have to worry about losing much money if you're testing small. If you're using direct mail, just mail a few thousand packages to your best customers. If the offer bombs, then you're out no more than several thousand dollars. If you test 10 of those ideas, obviously you're out several tens of thousands of dollars. **But let's say you get a positive response from Idea #11, and you invest another $20,000 into rolling it out big—and it's a phenomenal hit that earns you $1,000,000 in a few**

months. All of a sudden, you're not down $50,000; you're up $950,000. Better yet, the promotion will probably go on to make you even more money; and even after it peters out, you can reuse its very best elements in future tests and promotions.

Can you see how simple this is? Yet most people just don't understand this concept! **Most marketers are afraid to test new ideas because they're scared of losing money. I'm telling you to do the exact opposite of what those people do.** Now, you don't want to spend money frivolously or break the company on a loony idea, because that's just stupid. **But you can hedge your bets and still make a mint if you test small but aggressively, to a limited list of your very best customers.** Those people already like you, trust you, and want to do more business with you. Because of that, they'll buy products and services that nobody else will buy. So really, you're likely to recover your expenses even if something is otherwise a flop. Of course, if even they don't buy the item, run away from the idea as fast as you can!

Once you've tested a group of ideas to this small group, **take the very best promotions—the ones that made you lots more money than you spent—and roll those ideas out to the rest of your customer base.** If a particular idea still makes you big profits, begin promoting the offer to people who have never done business with you before as part of your new customer acquisition program.

In this way, your best customers become a risk-free testing ground. Keep testing your new promotions to that select list of your best customers, and you'll rarely have to worry about losing a single penny. I've been doing this for over two decades now; during that time, we've made hundreds of individual test offers to our best customers, and we've lost money on only a handful. **That's a few small losses versus *hundreds* of gains, plus a few cases where we at least broke even.**

Because our primary marketing method is direct mail, one of our formulas is very simple: we use Two-Step Marketing (which I've outlined previously) and try to achieve $1 million a month in sales. **We seek to get a 5% response on our initial offer, and then a 5% conversion on follow-up, with an average sale of $2,500.** We call this a 5 and 5. To achieve our million-dollar monthly goal, we have to send out 40,000 direct mail pieces every week.

Basically, we have to generate 2,000 leads every week from those 40,000 pieces of mail. **Out of those 2,000 leads, we want to convert 5% — 100 leads — to sales at an average of $2,500 each.** That comes to $250,000 per week; four times that is our monthly million. Simple enough, right? **It all boils down to converting just one-quarter of one percent of all our prospects to sales.**

Now comes the burning question: "What assumptions must prove true for the promotion to achieve this goal?" **We know we can mail 40,000 direct mail pieces a week to our market; that's a certainty.** Our market is enormous, and we have the best possible sources of mailing lists. These consist of people who haven't yet done business with us, but who have proven that they're serious about making more money by inquiring about or purchasing a low-cost business opportunity from one of our competitors.

That takes care of Step #1 of our plan. **Step #2 is asking ourselves, "What do we have to do to get 5% of those people to respond to our initial offer?" and then implementing our** best answers. In Step #3, we ask, **"What do we have to do to get 5% of** *those* **people to give us an average of $2,500 for the initial combination of products and services we're trying to sell them?"** All those questions have to be answered to the best of our ability before we begin testing.

So it starts with a series of assumptions that we make about our prospects; some would call this a business or marketing plan. We then attempt to prove that those assumptions are true in every way. We've been doing this for over two decades now, so it gets easier and easier; we know which products, services, and promotions have made us the most money in the past, so we have plenty of historical references to work from. **In addition, we constantly keep an eye on the market to see what's making the most money for other companies.** We itemize that data, studying it to see which of our competitors' ideas we can incorporate into our own marketing plans. **Then we prepare the best possible strategy based on that research.**

I spend a lot of time brainstorming all this with my key staff members, including my marketing director, my general manager, my sales manager, and his sales team. We throw our best ideas on the table and go back and forth, talking about all the various ways we can, first, develop promotions that will cause 5% of our prospects to respond to our initial step; and, second, create something so powerful that at least 5% of *those* people will willingly pay $2,500 for our initial product or service. **This formula generates ideas that we might not otherwise have considered if we didn't use the formula.**

Ultimately, we have to ask ourselves, "What's it going to take every week to get 100 brand new customers to give us

$2500 as fast as possible?" Since these people don't know or trust us, that's a huge challenge. Of course, the definition of a "challenge" is some difficulty in a job that's stimulating to the people engaged in it. **So we try to make it fun, and look at it as something to run towards, rather than a problem to run away from.**

Needless to say, none of this is easy. It takes a lot of work, and we have to be very careful about the ideas we put into play. **But it's worth the time and effort.** Start with the very best plan you can develop. Then test as many variations as possible as fast and inexpensively as possible. **Study your numbers, pick out the biggest winners, and roll out only with those.** If you do that, you can lose money on 90-95% your ideas, and *still* make millions of dollars.

Clearly, this is one of the most powerful marketing principles ever. **You don't have to worry about losing money when you take a chance, because you're not gambling everything at once.** This helps you separate the diamonds from all that mud and stone you encounter as you mine for success, and you also get the occasional ruby or emerald, or even a garnet or two—the ideas that do fairly well but don't hit the ball out of the park. All that's part of the success process, too.

Remember: all it takes is one big winner out of a whole stack of "losers" to succeed in the long run. **Not only does this let you take enormous risks and still play it safe at the same time, you can lose money on most efforts and *still* rollout to mega-wealth.** Think of the enormous power this gives you, and implement this strategy at once!

GOLDEN RULE TWENTY SIX:

Four Easy Pieces

It takes just four easy steps to build a marketing system that automatically generates huge, never-ending profits—an endless flow of automatic cash. The goal of every good marketing system you develop should be to:

1. **Pinpoint** the type of prospect most likely to become your best customer;

2. **Develop** a sales message designed to attract only that type of person;

3. **Create** a series of steps to attract and convert many of those people; and

4. **Implement** a series of steps to resell to those people again and again.

That's it: just four steps, each requiring specific thoughts and actions. All your effort is directed toward building the marketing system, and then hiring other people to maintain it and keep it running smoothly. **When you do this the correct way, these four steps build a marketing system that generates massive amounts of cash.** It's the next best thing to a free ATM that cranks out all of the money you want and need.

Let's look closer at **STEP #1**. Who is most likely to become your very best customer? Whenever I meet one of my best existing customers at an event, I ask them, "Where do I find another thousand people just like you?" I say it as a joke and they laugh and I laugh—but the truth is, it's not a joke to me at all. I really do want to find another 1,000, 10,000, or better yet, 100,000 people just like them. And so do you! **If you already have an established customer base of people who know you, like you, and trust you based on the business you've done with them before, your first question must always be, "How do I find *more* of those people?"**

Start by determining the common denominators those people share. We've been over these questions before: What things are most important to them? What are they searching for the most? What causes them to buy your products and services? Why have they done so much business with you in the past? Why have they done business with your biggest competitors? What are they searching for the most that they're finding the least? What causes them to re-buy as much as they do? **These are questions that lead to answers that lead to better questions that lead to better answers.** So start digging deeper.

You've got to be willing to endure some real confusion and frustration to get behind the eyeballs of these people, and figure out what makes them tick. What's most important to them? What frustrates them? What are their biggest problems and challenges? What are their greatest fears, failures and frustrations? How can you be the golden solution to all their biggest problems? These are also great questions to ask—and again, realize that the first answers you get won't be the best. **You have to keep asking and answering to dig as deeply as possible, so you can come up with your biggest breakthrough answers.**

The first step, then, continues for as long as you serve that particular marketplace. **You're going to keep asking the above**

questions and more: who is most likely to become your very best customer, and what can you give them that none of your competitors can? What can you do that will blow them away? What can you do that will shock them? What's bold and different and provides extreme value to them? **Take your very best answers and use them to implement Step #2.**

STEP #2 is to develop the very best sales message you can. Try to focus on your perfect customer and develop promotions around them, knowing that you want to attract and retain the maximum number of people who are just like them. You can pick a real person, or create a composite that you then give a name to. **Obviously, your very best sales messages are those that have the most appeal to them, things that will cut through their built-up sales resistance and the clutter of noise from other marketers.**

In order to do Step #2 well, you have to know and understand your marketplace in the most intimate sort of way. In order to do *that*, you have to become an avid student of your marketplace, including your competitors and all the products, services, and promotions that are making them the most money. This also requires a deep analysis of the people you're trying to sell to.

STEP #3 is to create a series of steps that attract the largest number of those people and get the highest possible percentage to buy from you right now. This requires a system of steps because the average prospect is extremely skeptical. On one hand, they sincerely desire the main benefits your product/ service line provides; but on the other, **you have to win their trust before they buy.** If you're selling a combination of products and services for $5,000, for example, **it's very hard to**

make a sale in one step. It usually requires a series of smaller steps or sales before they trust you enough to give you $5,000. **Accomplishing this involves a process of winning their hearts, and fully educating them on the extreme value of your products and services.**

If you don't know how to build a multi-step marketing system, my best advice is to get on the mailing lists of as many companies as possible who *are* using powerful multi-step marketing systems, and buy products and services from them. **Spending money to make more money has always been a classic business strategy, and in this case it helps you develop your marketing models** by emulating the most aggressive marketers in the field—those who are doing the best jobs at building turnkey marketing systems that convert the largest percentage of prospects to sales.

All you have to do is become one of their prospects. Inquire about or purchase the first step of their marketing system, and then hold out and *don't* buy for as long as possible—ideally, until they give up on you, which will take a while. **Closely observe the steps they use to try to make that initial big sale. This allows you to legally, morally, and ethically spy on them.** This works not just for those you compete with directly, but also with indirect competitors—**because a good marketing system can be adapted to any market.** Once you've observed the marketing systems of companies who have mastered the art and science of marketing, you'll have clues about how to develop your own.

STEP #4 is to create a system that makes it simple and easy to resell to existing customers for the longest period of time possible. All the money you want and need is out there right now in your marketplace, inhabiting the wallets, purses, and credit lines of potentially millions of people, assuming you've chosen the right marketplace. **Your goal must be to get as many of those people as you can to re-buy from you often enough for enough profit per transaction and with the maximum amount of efficiency.** That's how you make millions: simple but by no means easy, like so many other things in this field. But it does eventually become easier when you get good at building complete marketing systems that do all the selling and reselling for you.

Here at M.O.R.E., Inc., we have a weekly staff meeting where we discuss the status of our current promotions and plan new ones. Often our current promotions are working out smoothly, so there's no news to present. We then brainstorm ideas for new promotions we can initially test to our house list, spending 60-90 minutes at it. **Every month, we come up with two or three ideas we can all get excited about; these we test to our established customers.** If those ideas prove phenomenally successful, we can test them to the greater marketplace of people who haven't done business with us yet.

Our list of established customers (a.k.a. our house list) represents the bread-and-butter of our business. It keeps our doors open, keeps the profits flowing in, and acts as the ultimate proving ground for new products, services, or offers. **So our weekly meetings are themselves part of our system for developing new front-end customer acquisition promotions.** They encourage us to strategize and then implement the ideas and methods that ultimately become an important part of our overall marketing system.

Think deeply about all four of these steps. Each offers its own set of unique challenges, and that's definitely how you should think of this. **None of these issues are problems you run from; they're challenges you run *toward*, that you find interesting and exciting, that engage you, that can be enormously profitable.** All this can be systematized to bring you massive sales and profits on a consistent basis. Once you build the marketing system, all you have to do is find the most capable people you can to run it for you. Do that, and a fortune can come pouring in without you having to lift a finger.

At that point, you'll have the freedom and flexibility to spend your time developing new marketing systems. You become like one of those plate spinners you've seen on TV. A good plate spinner can have as many as 10-15 plates spinning at once; once they're up and running, it takes very little effort to walk up and down that line, maintaining their spin. That's a good visual analogy, I think, of **how you can have multiple marketing systems that keep producing sales and profits and require very little effort on your part to keep them rolling along.**

The Marketing Two-Step

In this chapter, I'll tell you all about a little-known two-step marketing approach that lets you create new products and services that sell like hotcakes on a cold winter morning. It's simple enough: **In Step #1, you make specific types of promises in your front-end lead generation promotion; in Step #2, you scramble to fill those promises on the back end.**

Your initial promises must be:

1. Big

2. Bold

3. Revolutionary

4. Unique

5. Exciting

6. New or new-sounding

All those things must apply. And again, it all comes down to knowing what's most important to your best prospects and customers. Now, the thing is, we talk a lot about the key to success being as simple as giving people what they want. **A "want" is simply an unfulfilled desire, still seeking fulfillment.**

In order for you to use this approach to developing profitable products and services, **you have to start by asking and answering some very deep questions, such as:** What are the five things that are most important to the best prospects in my market, and why? What are they searching for when they purchase and repurchase the types of products and services you sell? What benefits excite and interest them the most? What are their biggest problems and challenges? What would it take to solve those problems once and for all? Once you come up with a list of as many answers as possible, **the items on your list will lead you to the most revolutionary products and services you can invent—the kinds of things your best prospects will go crazy over.**

If you've been in business for a while, another great question for you to ask yourself is, **"What products and services have sold the very best for us in the past, and why?"** Really get to the heart of the matter. Your job is to dig deeper than any of your competitors are digging, and to think about all this in a much more serious way than they do. Spend more time and effort asking and answering these very difficult questions. To the degree that you do this, you'll get your breakthrough answers that can lead to massive profits—and that's the key to implementing this strategy.

You must think like a politician who desperately wants to get elected. In the first step, **you make bold promises to the people** you want to vote for you, and in the second you actually do what very few politicians ever do: **you seek a way to carry out those promises.** This can be extremely challenging, requiring a tremendous investment of time, work, energy, effort and money to accomplish. Yet the payoff can be huge.

Your big, bold, exciting promises must be woven into the very fabric of your lead generation sales materials, so they will compel the very best prospects to take an initial action that will lead to them taking a bigger action. In other words, you want them buy from you the first time and then re-buy again and again. **Because those promises must be centered around things that are important to them, you do have to dig much deeper than most of your competitors are willing to do.** You have to ask yourself those hard questions that they *refuse* to ask.

Keep the rewards firmly in mind as you move forward. In fact, fall in love with the game of marketing and innovation; when you do that, you'll gain a tremendous amount of satisfaction and personal fulfillment, as well as money. To me, asking and answering the questions I've just given you and then developing the products and services that fulfill on my big promises is the most exciting game on Earth. It's creative, challenging, and extremely rewarding, both personally and financially. I hope you can catch that vision.

Let's take a look at a few examples of how we're using this two-step approach at M.O.R.E., Inc. on a daily basis. **We sell business opportunities.** We have literally thousands of competitors who offer a wide variety of products, services, and opportunities to our marketplace. **The good news is that there's plenty of room in the marketplace, give the millions of prospective buyers searching for a powerful and proven low-cost way to become financially independent.**

The bad news is that we *do* have thousands of competitors, many of whom have advantages that we don't. Some outweigh us when it comes to resources; others are much smaller, so they have very little in the way of infrastructure, and can make excellent profits with poor percentages of response. Another problem is that all these competitors are trying to outshout to each other, and they're *all* coming up with bigger and bolder promises.

Each of our competitors tries to "out-promise" the others—and some of the claims we compete against are insane.

In order to succeed in this highly competitive marketplace, we're forced to use Step #1 very aggressively ourselves. We have to create the most revolutionary promises possible in order to attract the interest of our market's best prospects. We have to offer moneymaking opportunities that seem totally new, fresh, and exciting. **We must back our promises with as much proof as we can develop, so we can convince people that what we have for them is real, and lives up to all our promises.**

That forces us to constantly push the envelope, testing as many different ideas as possible as fast as we can to determine which will be the best received in our market. **It forces us to keep using proven marketing models that have worked well for us in the past.** In other words, we continue to re-run variations of the same promotions that have been successful before. We constantly look for new ways to reinvent them; that's the ultimate shortcut to quickly developing promotions that seem "new" and "different" and yet contain all the elements that have generated the most profits for us in the past. **After all, people want a taste of the familiar along with the new.**

In most cases, we can easily slot new products, services and ideas into existing models, while still giving our prospects the appearance of something revolutionary.

Every low-cost business opportunity we promote has three common components:

- A product or service.

- A cutting-edge system designed to automatically sell the product or service.

- The actual fulfillment of our marketing system and the materials that make it simple and easy for customers to use, or to prove to themselves that this opportunity is everything that we promised it was and more.

Within those three common denominators are hundreds of available choices. Over the years, we've tested so many different ideas that we have a working model that allows us to quickly and easily develop and then sell new moneymaking opportunities.

Nowadays, in Step #1 we use lead generation sales materials that make promises that are attractive to our marketplace. Most of those sales materials are for an advertising and management service we sell. Over the years, we've developed many different advertising and management services, but they all have the same basic features built into them. **Therefore, we can make the same basic promises in the first step; so we continue to use the same basic sales materials year after year.** We're constantly looking for products and services that will get our customers super-excited, items that are bold and different that we can then incorporate into our overall marketing model.

Our goal for many years has been to systematize all this, so we can keep speeding up the process of testing ideas and implementing the best results. Because we continue to add new twists to the same promotions over and over again, we can develop very elaborate and effective two-step marketing systems that do an effective job with both steps. Reusing proven marketing models offers you tremendous leverage; this is a wonderful shortcut to greater profits.

Here's what I mean: the first time you develop a complete two-step marketing system, it may take you hundreds or even thousands of person hours; **but every time you reuse it, you shorten that time dramatically.** Eventually, it might take you just a few dozen hours to develop and market a new product. We've even had some rare promotions where we've started marketing a new product in a day or two. It's not easy to do, but it's possible if you have plenty of experience and resources (especially in the form of earlier promotions) to draw upon. **This can be a tremendously effective 1-2 power punch.**

So constantly look for the biggest, boldest promises you can make to your best prospects. Dig as deep as you can into all the biggest reasons why people buy what you sell. **Remember, good marketing is psychology and math; that's all it is.** The psychology is where you get behind their eyeballs; you become them, you learn to think like them, you get inside their heads and hearts. **You try to experience what they're experiencing.**

For example: because I know that many of my best prospects and customers are constantly searching for new ways to make money, **I take entire days where I do nothing but go on the Internet and look at hundreds of competitor websites, pretending I'm a prospective buyer.** I fill out their questionnaires and surveys, I send for the free items they're offering, and I read all the hype they're publishing. I examine their wild and crazy promises, and I watch their videos.

After only a few hours of doing this, I'll be so frustrated and confused that it's painful. I experience the emotional suffering that my best customers are also experiencing, living my life through their eyes. **At that point, I'll stop and meditate on what I've seen. I'll think it all through, and end up understanding them in a much deeper way.** I internalized the problems that they go through in their quest for the very best moneymaking opportunities.

There are two basic kinds of knowledge: knowing something in your head, and knowing it in your heart. The best way is to know it in your heart. When you can do that, you *become* your best customer. **You think as they think; you experience the same problems and frustrations they experience.** If you do this enough, your understanding of the people in your marketplace will become much deeper. **Only then can you *really* know what kinds of promises you have to make to set yourself apart from your competitors.**

There's no way you can ever differentiate yourself from your competitors unless and until you thoroughly understand every aspect of your marketplace, including:

- Who your competitors are.

- The promises they're making to try to attract the same prospects as you.

- What they're doing right.

- What they're doing wrong.

- The common denominators all of them seem to be using.

That last point is essential, because the more you study your market, the more you'll see that many of your competitors are simply following the follower. They're all making the same tired, worn-out promises. They refuse to do any fresh, creative thinking.

Only when you pretend that you're a prospective buyer searching for the very best products and services in the marketplace, surfing hundreds of websites and sending away for a wide variety of information on every available choice you have, only when you've talked to a lot of sales reps and followed up on all those low-cost and no-cost information packages, **only when you're *seriously* trying to put yourself in your customers' place by weighing out all this evidence very carefully—only then can you truly understand what you have to do to separate yourself from your competition, and which promises you have to make to cut through the clutter rampant in your marketplace.** You'll also become very confused and frustrated during this process—just like your prospects. So be forewarned!

There will be times when you'll be pulling out your hair (which is why I have very little nowadays!). You have to go in with your eyes wide open, knowing that you'll experience plenty of confusion and frustration. But realize that it's all part of the price you must pay to develop your breakthrough ideas. **Only by subjecting yourself to a tremendous number of ideas can you know which of your ideas are better than all the others, which of your competitors do the best job of serving your prospects, and which are making the biggest mistakes.** And don't just limit yourself to your specific niche; be sure to evaluate the general marketplace as well, those other companies selling products or services that are completely unrelated to yours but which serve the same basic marketplace. **Try to determine what they're doing right or wrong, too.**

On top of that, look at the very best marketers in *every*

market. Study those who seem to be doing the most effective jobs at creating promises that persuade people to give them their money. There are so many sharp marketers out there nowadays, especially as the marketplace becomes overly competitive and over-saturated. **That forces the very best to rise to the top.** The more you study them, with the intention of learning everything you can, the better off you'll be in terms of inventing and implementing revolutionary marketing concepts and methods — because you'll be able to fuse their ideas with yours to create something altogether new.

Become a serious student of marketing. Study the broader market, not just your niche, for ideas and methods that you can use to cross-fertilize your own. The more you do this, the more common denominators you'll discover — common denominators that other people can't see. You'll also be able to spot those rare individuals and companies who are a cut above all the others, and who are already using these methods and strategies I've outlined here. **Once you can see who your real competitors are, and what they're doing to succeed, you'll have a terrific edge over *all* your competitors.**

So think deeply about this two-step approach to marketing. On the surface, it seems simple, and even easy: just make big, bold promises (Step #1), and then find every way you can to develop products and services that fulfill on those promises (Step #2). **And while it is in fact simple, in the sense that all great things are, it's not necessarily easy. I recommend that you view it as the ultimate challenge, the greatest game on Earth.** Actually learn to enjoy it, and you'll become like the mad scientist who works joyfully in the lab all day long, trying to discover that revolutionary breakthrough that catapults you to the top of your marketplace, making you massive sums of money for life!